Leave
Only
Paw Prints

Dog Hikes
in San Diego County

Leave Only Paw Prints

Dog Hikes in San Diego County

By Donna Lawrence

"Adventures in the Natural History and Cultural Heritage of the Californias"

SUNBELT PUBLICATIONS
San Diego, California

Leave Only Paw Prints: Dog Hikes in San Diego County
Sunbelt Publications, Inc

Edited by Jennifer Redmond
Cover design by Kathleen Wise
Cover background image © ShutterStock, Inc.
Composition by Jack Brandais
Project management by Jennifer Redmond
Anza-Borrego Desert State Park, California State Parks and park logos are regis-tered trademarks of California State Parks
Printed in the United States of America

Sunbelt Publications, Inc.
P.O. Box 191126
San Diego, CA 92159-1126
(619) 258-4911, fax: (619) 258-4916
www.sunbeltbooks.com

10 09 08 07 06   5 4 3 2 1

"Adventures in the Natural History and Cultural Heritage of the Californias"
A Series Edited by Lowell Lindsay

Library of Congress Cataloging-in-Publication Data

Lawrence, Donna.
Leave only paw prints : dog hikes in San Diego County / by Donna Lawrence. — 1st ed.
    p. cm.
Includes index.
ISBN-13: 978-0-932653-78-9
ISBN-10: 0-932653-78-2
1. Hiking with dogs—California—San Diego County—Guidebooks. 2. Trails—California—San Diego County—Guidebooks. 3. San Diego County (Calif.)—Guidebooks. I. Title.

SF427.455.L39 2004
796.5109794'98—dc22

                                                        2006009685

All photographs are from the author's collection.

Contents

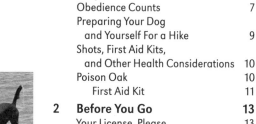

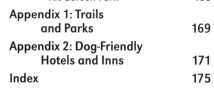

Bob Lawrence and Bailey on the trail at Los Peñasquitos.

Preface

As any dog owner knows, a dog is part of the family. He (or she) is not a possession. Even though we say dog "owner," Fido ranks right up there with the humans. The family unit may consist of parents, kids, and a dog, or it may be just people and a dog, with no kids. Many dog owners sign their dog's name to holiday cards and celebrate their pooch's birthday. Canines are called man's best friend for good reason. We feel they understand us and love us unconditionally. They relate to us in ways no other pet does. (Note to cat owners: Sorry. This is my opinion and the opinion of other dog owners. It does not reflect the opinion of anyone who has not owned a dog.)

As close as we feel to our dogs, it is natural that we want to take them along on our travels. Whether we are leaving for a day or a week, we tend to want to bring along our canine pals. Taking them with us not only means we don't have to leave them alone for the day or board them in a kennel, but also that we can enjoy their zest for life. We watch their pure joy in being outside, being with us, and discovering the larger world. Their happiness magnifies our pleasure in the experience. The problem is, there are people who do not share our affection for dogs and do not welcome them. The purpose of this book is to discover places throughout San Diego County where you are welcome to take your dog to hike, romp, and play.

Along with nearly year round sunshine, the county offers a wide range of environments to enjoy with your pet, from mountain forests to ocean beaches to vast desert. In addition, there are numerous dog parks and sunny urban walks where canines can accompany you while you roam the city.

This book offers detailed descriptions of nature hikes in the mountains, hillsides, canyons, and deserts of this large county. It also introduces you to the leash-free dog parks and beaches. For visitors to the San Diego area, the Appendix features a list of hotels that welcome pooches.

Paw Prints

Many of us are familiar with the words, "Take only memories, leave only footprints," and its variations, "Take only photographs (or pictures), leave only footprints." For anyone taking a dog to a wilderness area, a beach, or a park, "Leave only paw prints" is a natural extension of this. It reflects common courtesy, as well as a respect for the land and for the people who will follow.

The City of San Diego has adopted this phrase, "Leave only paw prints," as a reminder, posted on signs at all of its dog parks and beaches. It is also used in other parts of the country — at a nature preserve in West Virginia, at dog beaches in Maryland, and no doubt in other places where people love dogs and appreciate the natural environment.

When I saw the sign at my first visit to a dog park, it made me smile. It is a lovely, succinct way of stating both a dog-friendly and land-friendly philosophy.

Acknowledgments

I want to thank all of the dog owners I spoke with on trails, in dog parks, and on dog beaches. So many were happy to share with me their favorite dog destinations. I enjoyed their companionship and was delighted at the playfulness and good behavior of their pets. Some, like Max at Morley Field Dog Park, even invited me to play by pushing a ball into my hand as I was talking with another dog's owner.

I am also grateful to the helpful staff at California State Parks,

Bailey poses with the author.

like Heide Addison, a ranger at Cuyamaca Rancho State Park, who clued me in on places to go in that park. She is always looking for good places to walk her dog. Thanks go to the staff at the City of San Diego Park and Recreation Department, to Linda Carson at the Anza-Borrego Foundation, Anabele Cornejo at the Cleveland National Forest offices, Chris Nyce at the Palomar Ranger District, Amy Harbert at the San Diego County Parks and Recreation Department, and to many others who answered my questions along the way.

A special thank you goes to Jack Brandais, my cat-loving friend and author of *Weekend Driver San Diego*, who suggested I might write this book — and even designed it.

And to my husband Bob, thank you for hiking with me, helping wrangle Bailey, and for always letting me know you love and appreciate me.

Bailey is always ready to take off.

Introduction

In the 1960s, novelist John Steinbeck drove a camper truck along the back roads of this country with a large French poodle named Charley as his only travel companion, then he wrote *Travels With Charley*, a tale of a matter-of-fact dog lover. He didn't gush; he wrote about his dog as if he were a human friend. I can understand that. Charley provided company for Steinbeck, sometimes entertainment, and frequently introduced him to folks along the road. Steinbeck was determined to become reacquainted with America, and he found, as most dog owners know, that a friendly dog is often a connection to other people.

Strangers more readily talk to strangers who have a dog on a leash.

Steinbeck's Charley was always ready for the next trip. Does that sound like your dog? Does he want to jump in the car with you wherever you go? Does he make you feel guilty if you close the front door with him still inside?

Our dog Joey, who lived with us for 16 years, did not like to travel. He was a Peek-a-Poo, a sweet-faced combination of Pekinese and Poodle, who tended to get carsick whenever we took him along on a trip. Although he did not like to see us go out the door, he would, it seemed, just curl up and wait for our return. He was our dear friend and a good watchdog, but a road companion — never.

Bailey in a rare quiet moment.

A couple of years after we lost Joey, we began to visit local animal shelters, hoping to fall in love again. We were not certain what we were looking for. Our only determination was that we would get a shorthaired dog this time. Joey shed badly, and we did not want to comb up blond fur from the carpet anymore. We saw many eager dogs at the shelters, most of them large. We had always had a small dog before, and I did not feel that I would be comfortable with a large dog, even though I knew many that were really wonderful pets. There were a few small pups in the shelters, but not the one that we knew we had to take home.

Finally, on a return visit to the Lake Elsinore Animal Shelter, we saw the one. There he was, blond, longhaired, disheveled, and adorable. Two young volunteers were gingerly combing through his thick coat. He immediately wiggled his way into our hearts—so much for our getting a shorthaired dog this time. He was a mix, largely Havanese. We held him, walked him, talked to him, and put in our claim to adopt him. A week later, we picked him up, brought him home and named him Bailey.

Soon after we got Bailey home, we realized that he is a traveler. He loves to go. When he sees the leash, he chases his tail madly in happy anticipation. His exuberance is unmistakable.

Even on a leash, he leaps with joy as he takes off after a rabbit or some imagined creature in the park. When he is in the car, he watches out the window constantly, not wanting to miss anything. I felt I owed it to Bailey to find out where in San Diego County I could take him for exercise and fresh air. Lots of people take their dogs on hikes and to parks and beaches. It seemed like a wonderfully companionable thing to do. (I had no idea what a challenge that would present with Bailey.)

Where We Go

This book covers hikes in the mountain wilderness in the Cleveland National Forest, Palomar Mountain State Park, and Cuyamaca Rancho State Park. We explore Anza-Borrego Desert State Park in a separate section. Then we visit some of the many regional parks in the county that can take you back to nature, while you are still in or near the city. Some of these are San Diego City Regional Parks and Open Spaces, some are San Diego

Botanical Trail at the Elfin Forest Recreational Reserve.

Batiquitos Lagoon trail has places to stop and rest.

County Parks, and some are regional parks in other communities around the county. These range from walks by lagoons to hikes through steep chaparral-covered hillsides. Then we go to the many leash-free dog parks in San Diego and other nearby cities. Turning to the coast, we will enjoy the four leash-free dog beaches in the county. And then we take a walk in the park (on leash) in several of the local spots where you can share a beautiful San Diego day with your pet.

A note to owners of female dogs: the dogs I have owned have all been males, so I am accustomed to saying he. I am using the male pronoun in this book to avoid the awkward he/she construction. Please accept my apologies to Mitzi, Fifi, Ginger, and all of your other sweet female dogs. Whenever I say he, I also mean she.

Trail Advisories

For the trails through mountain, desert, and hillside, we have signs at the beginning of each trail description to give you an idea of the difficulty of the hike. Some trails start out easy and then have more strenuous sections. I have tried to give you an idea of the terrain you will be encountering. Easy generally means that the trail is fairly level, with perhaps a little uphill or downhill. These are my evaluations of the difficulty. If you are a marathon runner, what I find strenuous you might find moderate. The dog parks, beaches, and urban walks are not rated. They are, after all, a walk in the park.

Let's go, let's go, let's go!

Part One: Traveling With Your Dog

Any trip involves planning, and a trip with your dog requires some additional preparation if it is to be a happy experience for all. First you need to determine whether this particular trip is really an appropriate one for your furry companion. You know your dog best. If your destination requires a long driving trip, is he a good and patient passenger? Or does he bound endlessly from one side of the car to the other and bark at passing motorcycles? Will your dog be welcome, or at least tolerated, when you get there? (Don't assume. Call, fax, or e-mail to be certain.) Are you prepared to handle the demands of dog care on the road?

If you are planning a wilderness trip, whether for camping or for a day hike, be sure that the trails you pick are not too arduous for your dog. If he is normally confined to a small yard, with occasional

walks around the block, he may not be ready to climb Palomar Mountain.

One of San Diego County's attractions is its warm weather, but can also be a drawback. Check weather reports. If afternoon temperatures are expected to soar, plan your hike for early in the day or late afternoon. You will all be more comfortable. Remember that dogs are as susceptible as humans to heat stroke. And they cannot take off their fur coats.

A hike across a creek at Los Peñasquitos Canyon Preserve.

1 Preparations

Obedience Counts

If you are going to take your dog with you anywhere, it is essential that he be obedient. Basic training is necessary. Your pooch should stay, sit, and come when you call, at the very least. The dog parks and dog beaches that allow you to take him off the leash require that your pet respond to simple voice commands from you. He must be able to handle encounters with other animals and people in a safe and civilized manner. If your dog is aggressive toward other dogs, you cannot let him off leash, even at an approved off-leash park or beach.

In most of the places you take your dog, he will be on a leash. But even then, he must be socialized enough to not bark at people passing by or pull wildly trying to attack another animal. When hiking on trails, you never know what may appear around the next bend. You may suddenly come across other hikers, equestrians, mountain bikers, rattlesnakes, or other surprises. Your short leash will help you keep your dog close, but you need to stay aware of your surroundings and try to head off any possible confrontations. When you are on a narrow trail and see someone approaching, it is good etiquette to pull your dog in close and step off to the right, to avoid blocking the path.

Unfortunately, Bailey was not socialized when we brought him home. He quickly adjusted to us as his family and to our home as his territory. He was affectionate from the start and wanted to sit on our laps or lie next to us, maintaining physical contact.

Enjoying Fiesta Island.

He gave us his complete trust. But he was hostile toward anyone passing by. Other dogs, skateboarders, and motorcycles drove him crazy. A walk in the neighborhood park became a frenzy if there was another dog in sight. Bailey needed training.

There are numerous dog training books available, if you want to handle the training yourself. Starting when your dog is a puppy is always best, of course. Puppies learn faster than older dogs, who may have already established bad behavior patterns. But, as with Bailey, it may be too late for early training. I don't know how old Bailey was when he came to live with us. The shelter estimated his age to be three or four years. He may have been younger than that, but he had already developed some bad behaviors. We started working on Bailey's training ourselves, and he made some progress. He still needed some socialization, so we hired a trainer to come to our home and teach us how to train Bailey. We have taken Bailey along on many of our hikes for this book. Other times he was left at home. At this writing, I would not take him to any of the leash-free parks, because he cannot be trusted to reliably respond to my voice command. But when I visited those parks, I was encouraged by the many dogs who can play together and respond when their owner calls.

We are still working on socializing Bailey, and I look forward to many more walks with him in the places described in this book. He has responded to our efforts at training. We know that we need to be consistent and persistent. It is worth it, having a pet who is not only happy with us, but also with others.

If you have a young dog, obedience classes provide a good way to get him used to being around other dogs and people. And as mentioned above, there are also trainers who will work with you individually on specific problems. Whether you train your dog yourself, or get help, it is important to give him the opportunity to be around other people and dogs frequently, so he will become accustomed to this.

It is your responsibility as a dog owner to have a well-behaved dog that is not a threat or a nuisance to anyone. Besides, it will make the time spent out in the world with your fuzzy friend much more enjoyable.

Preparing Your Dog and Yourself For a Hike

If you plan to take your dog on a wilderness hike in the mountains or the desert, you both need to be in condition for it. A daily walk around the block does not prepare either of you for an eight-mile trek.

Before going on a hike of a significant length, practice some endurance training for both of you. Don't do it all at once. If you usually take a ten-minute walk with your dog, gradually increase it to half an hour. Watch how your dog is reacting. If he is panting or slowing down, find some shade and let him rest. Even during your

Trail at Palomar Mountain State Park.

training walks, start carrying water with you. You both need to stay hydrated. If he is still pulling ahead at half a mile, work your walk up to a mile. Include hills if possible. After the two of you have built up your endurance together, you will have a good idea of how long and how far you can go with your pet.

For the hikes I discuss in the wilderness and the desert, I do not recommend any specific length for a hike. You need to decide what you and your dog are comfortable with. If you are both experienced hikers, you can take on the more ambitious trails. For others there are plenty of one- to two-mile hikes. Some routes loop around and return to the starting point. If the route you choose does not loop, be sure to turn around and head back when you have covered about half of your desired distance. Remember that you need to cover the same ground coming back.

Shots, First Aid Kits, and Other Health Considerations

First Aid Kit

- Elastic bandage
- Scissors
- Adhesive tape
- Band-Aids
- Antibiotic cream
- Aspirin
- Tweezers
- Hydrogen peroxide
- Sunblock
- Pre-moistened hand wipes
- Moleskin

Before you take your dog to a dog park or on a wilderness hike, be sure his shots are up to date. Check with your vet if you are not certain when booster shots are due.

A first aid kit with items for you and your pet can allow you to take care of minor problems before you get home. Even if you are just out on a day hike, a basic kit is advisable.

Some people use a DEET-free insect repellant on their dogs as well as themselves. This can help guard against ticks, which can carry Lyme Disease, and mosquitoes, which can carry West Nile Virus. (For yourself, use sunblock before you start on your hike, and reapply if you are out in the sun for several hours.)

If your dog has long hair, take his brush in the car, so you can gently brush out burrs and other prickly things.

Remember that when you are hiking, or even at a park or beach, if you are hot, your dog is too. The combination of heat and overexertion can be serious. If your dogs shows signs of heat exhaustion, such as excessive panting, vomiting, weakness, stumbling, or glassy eyes, get him into the shade. Cool down his head and body by rubbing him gently with cool water. Let him rest in the shade until he perks up. It would be best to cut the hike short at this point. If you have to find shade and rest along the way back, do.

Poison Oak

Poison oak is common in southern California's natural areas. It is actually a shrub, with leaves in clusters of three. You should learn to recognize it and keep your dog and yourself out of it. If your dog makes contact with it he may develop an itchy rash. You will see him chewing at his paws or scratching at his ears. Even if your dog shows no signs of having been affected, the poison may be on his fur. When you touch him, you may find yourself with the rash.

If you suspect that your pet has gotten into poison oak, try not to touch him with bare hands until you can get him into a bath. Wear rubber gloves to shampoo him. For you, calamine lotion or an over-the-counter cortisone cream can help ease the itching, if it is not too severe.

Bailey is ready to go.

2 Before You Go

Your License, Please

Just as you need a driver's license to drive, your dog needs a dog license. And he should always be wearing it on his collar. Dog licensing is usually a function of the city in which you live. It is not expensive, and it is required. Most parks, beaches, and wilderness areas that allow dogs insist that they wear their current license tags.

An additional identification tag with your dog's name, address, and telephone number, can help him to get back home if you become separated. (Okay, your dog doesn't have a telephone. You know what I mean.) You do not anticipate losing track of your dog, but unexpected things can happen.

If you have a computer-age dog, he may already have an embedded microchip to identify him if he gets lost. The animal shelter insisted on one for Bailey before we took him home. It was inserted just below the skin, between his shoulder blades. If you lose your dog and his collar comes off or is taken off, then a tag on the collar no longer helps. The microchip identification is permanent and is a reliable way for your dog's identification always to stay with him.

What to Take Along

For a day trip or a hike of several hours, your needs are fairly simple. A backpack can carry all of your necessities easily. First, of course, is water, enough for everyone on the trip, including pets. I have an insulated canteen with a shoulder strap that makes it easy to carry along. A small plastic bowl or a collapsible bowl will assure that your dog can get as much water as he needs. Although we allow Bailey to lap water from a bottle, we always pour some into a bowl as well.

Second, apply sunblock on any people coming on the hike, and carry the sunblock in your pack to reapply after a couple of hours. A DEET-free insect repellant for you and your dog is a good idea as well.

If you expect to be out for more than a few hours, bring some high-energy food for yourself and treats for your dog. Many of the hiking areas also have places for picnics. Even if they don't, a rest and a snack will provide a good break. Keep any snacks in a sealed container, so the odor of them will not attract unwanted trail mates.

In southern California, it is always a good idea to dress in layers. You can layer for warmth if you start early, in the cool morning hours, then take off sweaters or over shirts as the day warms up. I like to keep covered with a light long-sleeved shirt, even when it gets warm, to keep the sun off my arms. And with the bright, glaring sun, a hat and sunglasses are nearly always needed.

If your trip will be overnight, or over several nights, there are other considerations. Many dog owners endorse the use of crates when traveling overnight with their pet. If the dog gets used to the crate at home, then he will feel safer and more at home while on the road. This also makes your life easier if you are staying at a hotel. Note: If a hotel is your stopping over place, always call ahead to be sure that they allow dogs in the rooms. Sometimes policies change.

If you are going camping, plan ahead where your pet is going to sleep. In the tent with you? In the vehicle? Can you trust that he will be quiet during the night and not disturb other campers

Always make time for a drink.

or the nocturnal animals? If you are traveling in a recreational vehicle, you are taking part of your home with you, so that should accommodate everyone in the family.

In addition to your normal camping and cooking gear, be sure to take plenty of plastic bags for trash and all waste. Regular campgrounds will have trash containers, but if you are hiking, they may not be available. Remember, leave only paw prints (and footprints). Another slogan you will see on the trail is: "Pack it in, pack it out."

When packing for an overnight trip, do not forget the dog food, a food dish, and your pet's favorite toys, and you should be ready to go.

When you are going to a wilderness or desert area, always get maps of the area. Visitor's centers and ranger's offices can be very helpful with information on trails, facilities, and conditions of roads. Check the weather reports for your destination before you leave.

Water, Water, Water

It bears repeating: the most important thing to take along when you travel with your dog in southern California is water, whether you are on a hike or just enjoying a few hours at the beach or park. Take plenty of water for yourself and for your dog. Whether your dog will lap water from a tipped bottle, or only from a bowl, be prepared. Collapsible bowls (available at pet supply stores) can be put in your backpack for a water break. Or, for a very inexpensive travel bowl, a zipper-type plastic sandwich bag, with the top folded over, will become a bowl of sorts if you pour a couple of inches of water into it. When your dog has lapped his fill, you can dump out anything left and fold it back up again for easy carrying.

Do not let your dog drink from streams or ponds (and do not drink from them yourself). These water sources may be contaminated. They can contain bacteria and parasites that cause serious gastric problems. *Giardia lamblia* is one nasty parasite that is picked up from drinking contaminated water. The resulting Giardiasis can cause vomiting, diarrhea, and bloating. If you notice these symptoms in your dog, get him to the vet.

When you are at the beach and there is a brisk ocean breeze, it is easy to forget that your dog is getting hot as he runs after that Frisbee. During a vigorous workout, you should periodically offer him water breaks. And have a drink of water yourself—dehydration is not good for any of us.

Leash Laws

On public property within cities, and in city, county, and state parks, and national forests, it is illegal to have your dog off leash,

Dogs must be leashed at all times
SDMC 63.02.2
Clean up after your pet
SDMC 44.0304.1

unless you are in a specified off-leash area. Most of these places require that a leash be no more than six or eight feet long, so that you can maintain control of your pet. If you are caught walking with your dog without a leash, you can be fined.

If you are heading to an off-leash dog park or beach, you must keep you dog on a leash while you are walking to the off-leash area. One dog owner at Nate's Point, an off-leash area in Balboa Park, told me that he was stopped and received a stern warning for not having his dog's leash fastened while they were walking to Nate's Point. It could easily have been a fine.

Even if you know your dog will stay with you and will respond to your voice command, the leash law is still the law.

Along Observatory Trail in the Cleveland National Forest.

Part Two: Parks in the Wild
State Parks, National Forests, and Preserves

Introduction to Wilderness Hikes

A **walk in the woods with** your dog at your side, both of you breathing in the pine-scented air, frolicking over rocks, and following trails through the wilderness is an idyllic scene. But dogs are prohibited in many wilderness park areas. There are exceptions — places where you and your pet can enjoy the mountains and forests together. We will be discussing these in the following chapters.

San Diego County's mountains are part of the Peninsular Range that starts in the north with the Santa Ana Mountains in Orange County, includes the San Jacinto Mountains in Riverside County, and the Palomar, Cuyamaca, and Laguna Mountains in San Diego County. From here the Peninsular Range continues southward into Baja California, forming the spine of the Baja peninsula. Large sections of these mountains that trend northwest to southeast diagonally across San Diego County are preserved and managed by the U.S. Forest Service, as part of the Cleveland National Forest. The national forest sits alongside two of our county's state parks, Palomar Mountain State Park and Cuyamaca Rancho State Park, in fact, surrounding these much smaller state parks.

The lower portions of these mountains, particularly those slopes facing west, have the familiar chaparral vegetation that covers so much of southern California. Canyons and the banks of streams may be rich with riparian growth, including tall oaks, sycamores, willows, and thick cattails. Higher up on the mountains, pine and cedar forests take over, giving some of these areas the look of the Sierra Nevada.

A richness of wildlife lives in these mountains, usually hidden from humans. From the trails you may see mule deer, gray foxes or coyotes. You almost certainly will see squirrels, rabbits, lizards, butterflies, and countless types of birds. You probably will not see mountain lions or black bears, although they do live in these mountains.

So, where can you go with your pet?

Dogs are allowed on a leash anywhere in the national forests. (They are not allowed in the National Parks, but we do not have any National Parks in San Diego County.) In California state parks,

Beautiful day at Lake Cuyamaca.

Picnic spot off the Inaja Memorial Trail.

like Palomar Mountain and Cuyamaca Rancho, dogs are allowed in specified areas only, and then they must be leashed. One reason leashes are important in wilderness areas is so that you can keep your pet from harming or harassing wildlife or other hikers. You also have a better chance of protecting him from being hurt.

A brochure put out by California State Parks warns that occasionally, dogs in wilderness areas may be killed by mountain lions or bears. That is enough to scare some of us right out of the wilderness ourselves. In reality, although hikers do occasionally see mountain lions (and even bears) in the parks, the appearance of these animals is rare. Even so, it is good to know some techniques to avoid confrontation with these large predators.

Facing Down Lions

The California Department of Fish and Game has published a free pamphlet called *Living With Mountain Lions*. It has instructions on what to do if you encounter a mountain lion (also known as a puma or cougar) to reduce the chance of an attack. First, do not hike alone. Travel in groups, and be sure to have enough adults to supervise the number of children. Keep the children close to you. Do not allow them to wander off. If you see a lion, give it a way to escape — don't approach it. And do not give in to the impulse to run away. Running will only make the lion want to chase you. Instead, stand tall and face it. Make eye contact. Try to appear as large as your can. Raise your arms and wave them slowly. If you are wearing a jacket, open it. Speak in a loud voice. You are trying to convince the mountain lion that you are not their prey and you may even be a danger to them.

If you have small children with you when you see a lion, try to pick up the children without crouching down or bending over. If you bend over, you look more like the type of animal they are prone to attack. Lions usually try to bite the head or neck of their prey. That is why it is important to remain standing and facing the animal. If the lion attacks, fight back. People have successfully fought off mountain lions with rocks, sticks, and other objects. For a copy of the pamphlet, you can call (916) 445-0411, request it by mail at California Department of Fish and Game, 1416 9th Street, Sacramento, 95814, or read it online at *www.dfg.ca.gov/lion/index.html*.

How to Avoid Bears

Black bears also live in our San Diego County forests, but seeing one is quite rare. Their name is misleading, since they are not always black; they are sometimes brown or a cinnamon color, and they may have a patch of white on their chest. The black bear is the only species of bear still living in California. The grizzly bear survives only on our state flag.

The San Diego Natural History Museum has a field guide on its web site with information on the flora and fauna you will most likely see on your hikes around the county. As part of this, they have tips on how to avoid close encounters of the bear kind. And what to do if you see a bear.

First, if you are camping or picnicking, in order to avoid attracting bears, keep your food and garbage in sealed containers. This includes dog food. You want to eliminate the odor of food. The idea is that you want to smell like the forest, not like lunch.

Never feed bears and don't leave food for them. This can make them associate humans with food. If you see a bear, keep your distance. If the bear is standing, it is not threatening you. It is surveying its surrounding.

If a bear approaches you, do not run. As with the mountain lions, running may cause them to run after you. Make sure the

Out for a day in the Cleveland National Forest.

bear has a clear retreat. Keep your dog close to you, on the leash. Make a lot of noise and throw things at the bear to distract its attention. If the bear continues approaching you, keep facing it while backing away slowly.

For further information from the San Diego Natural History Museum web site, go to *www.sdnhm.org.*

General Tips for Hikes With Pooch

Know your dog. Be aware of how he reacts to other critters. The six-foot leash will make it easier for you to control your dog if he is startled by a wild animal and turns into a snarling frenzy of fur.

You probably take your dog on walks on a leash frequently at home, so you know how he reacts when he spots local wildlife and other dogs and walkers. Pay attention to his behavior, in case there are any bad habits you need to work on with him. If your best friend displays aggressive behavior when meeting someone on the street, you cannot expect a different reaction on a wilderness trail. Work with him. If that does not work, take him to an obedience class or to a private trainer to help socialize him.

If you and your dog regularly take long walks, then you are both probably in good shape for many of the trails. But if his usual exercise is a brisk run around the backyard, get him into condition before your trip. Take moderate walks for a week or so, then increase the distance until you feel certain that a wilderness hike will not be too strenuous for either of you.

When you are preparing for a trip to a state park or national forest, bring a daypack with water for pooch and water for you. As mentioned earlier, many pet stores carry foldable water dishes that will stash neatly in your pack and pop open when you need them. A sealed plastic bag with dog treats or dry food is advisable if you plan to be out for several hours.

San Diego County mountains can get very warm in the daytime and can also cool down abruptly. Be prepared for either extreme of weather. Dressing yourself in layers is a good way to deal with that. As for your dog, since you cannot remove his fur coat in the heat, keep an eye on his level of comfort. If he appears overheated, find a patch of shade and get out that water. After he has lapped up his fill, let him rest before you take him back on the hot trail.

Pups take a ride near the Laguna Campground.

3 Cleveland National Forest

Introduction to National Forests

The U.S. Forest Service is very friendly toward dogs. Leashed dogs are permitted on trails anywhere within the forest boundaries. The leash should be no longer than six feet, so that you can maintain control of your pet. You cannot allow him to roam free.

Forest Service policy advises that if your dog is vicious or if he barks a great deal, leave him home. You need to observe courtesy toward other hikers and campers. They have a right to enjoy the forest without having to put up with your friend's noise. So Bailey is not going on any hikes in the forest with us just yet. Maybe he will be able to hike with us in the future, after he has had more training. Meanwhile, he stays home.

Forest Service officials also request that you bring no more than two dogs into the forest. This again is out of consideration

Along Lightning Ridge Trail.

for other hikers and campers. If you are camping with your dog, you need to keep him inside a vehicle or tent at night.

While you are hiking with your dog in the national forest, stay alert for posted signs that indicate you are leaving the national forest and entering either private property or a state park. Dogs are permitted only in specified areas in the state parks.

Permits

The Forest Service, which is part of the U.S. Department of Agriculture, charges fees for use of the national forests. The funds from these fees provide for maintenance of facilities and trails. There are several types of permits available for specific circumstances.

The Adventure Pass covers the basic fees for national forests in southern California, including Angeles, Cleveland, Los Padres, and San Bernardino national forests. At this writing, the one-day Adventure Pass is $5, the annual Adventure Pass is $30, and an Adventure Pass to put on a second vehicle is $5. These passes are either hangtags or peel-off bumper stickers.

The Golden Passes cover basic fees for any national forest or national park in the country. The annual Golden Eagle Pass is $65. The Golden Senior Pass is $10 for a lifetime pass. And the Golden Access Pass is free for those who are permanently disabled. By 2007, a new pass, called the America the Beautiful Pass, will be available. The details on that are not yet available.

In December 2004, the Federal Lands Recreation Enhancement Act was passed, setting a revised fee structure. The Adventure Pass is still the pass to buy for the Cleveland National Forest, but it is only needed for developed sites. If there are no

Forest Information

Brochures, maps, and other information are available at Cleveland National Forest offices. They are open 8 a.m. to 5 p.m. Monday-Friday.

- **Main Office**
  10845 Rancho Bernardo Road, Suite 200
  San Diego, CA 92127
  (858) 673-6180.

- **Alpine, Descanso, and Laguna Mountain areas**
  Descanso Ranger District
  3348 Alpine Boulevard
  Alpine, CA 91901
  (619) 445-6235

- **Palomar Mountain, Henshaw, Ramona and Oak Grove**
  Palomar Ranger District
  1634 Black Canyon Rd.
  Ramona, CA 92065
  (760) 788-0250

restrooms, picnic tables, or campsites, then you do not need an Adventure Pass to enter. If it is developed, then you need the pass. The Golden Passes still cover entrance to all of the national parks and forests. Both the Adventure Passes and the Golden Passes cover entrance fees, and they cover maintenance of picnic facilities, day-use facilities, restrooms, and trails. You may be charged an additional recreational fee for overnight camping and "high-impact recreation areas." When in doubt, check with the local ranger's office. Their addresses and phone numbers are listed in the sidebar.

The Golden Eagle Passports can be purchased by phone (877-465-2727) or online at *www.natlforests.org*. You can also get them at the Forest Service office and at ranger district offices. The Golden Age Pass and the Golden Access Pass must be purchased in person, at one of the offices. They are not available online.

Adventure Passes are available by phone (909-382-2622), at Forest Service ranger district offices, or through private vendors, including many sporting goods stores. Check the web site at *www.fs.fed.us/r5/sanbernardino/ap/index.php* to see where, or call your local sports store.

Trail Conditions

The national forests are, by definition, wilderness areas, and conditions can change from time to time, due to fires, flooding, rockslides, or extreme weather. Sometimes a trail may be closed for maintenance or because of some temporary dangerous condition. It is always a good idea to check with the Forest Service before heading for a hike in the forest. The web site for the Cleveland National Forest has a colored meter indicating fire danger and a link to click for information on current conditions. This tells you about specific trail and road closings. The web site for the Cleveland National Forest is at *www.fs.fed.us/r5/cleveland/*.

National Forest Tips for Hikers

The Forest Service offers tips that are useful wherever you are hiking. Regarding hiking with your dog, they note that you should watch for injuries to your pet's footpads when hiking rocky or extremely hot terrain. This is good advice. If your dog starts limping, pay attention and tend to it right away. If it is not something you can fix in the field, like pulling out a burr, you may have to carry your furry friend back down the trail.

They also advise that you travel with a companion, and that means a human companion, in addition to your pooch. Two or more people can look out for each other and one can go for help, if the other is injured. You should leave your itinerary with someone at home, along with your car make and license number. This is advisable even for a day trip into wilderness areas.

It is a good idea to get trail maps and topographic maps if you are hiking into the wilderness. These can be obtained from ranger offices. Some are available online.

Note regarding trail ratings: these ratings are my ratings and are, of course, subjective. If you are an experienced mountain climber, what I find moderate to strenuous, you may find easy. This is just to give you an idea of what to expect on these trails.

Trail Hikes

Observatory Trail
Backcountry

Trail
Easy To Moderate

Palomar Mountain's Observatory Trail is a fun, if somewhat ambitious way to get from the Observatory Campground to the famous Palomar Observatory. Your dog can accompany you on the trail, although not inside the observatory. The trail rises about 800 feet in elevation along its two miles. Or, you can start at the top of the trail, just outside the gates to the observatory, and go downhill to the campgrounds.

Directions

Take Interstate 15 to Highway 76 east. Follow this highway about 20 miles, to County Highway S-6 north. From here you wind around curves, gaining altitude with each turn, until you reach 5,000 feet. Pass the junction with County Highway S-7. You will see signs indicating that you go straight ahead for the observa-

World-famous Palomar Observatory.

tory and Observatory Campground. From the intersection, it is 3 miles to the campgrounds, 5 miles to the observatory. The campgrounds entrance is on the right.

Description

When you enter a national forest campground, if you do not have a valid Adventure Pass or Golden Pass, you need to pay the $12 day rate. There are envelopes and a place to put your payment. Keep the tear-off permit on your dashboard.

Drive halfway around the campgrounds road to the opposite side. We spotted a small gray fox trotting across the road here.

You will find parking spaces and a sign for the amphitheater and the Observatory Trail.

Once on the trail, you are into the woods, with huge pines, oak, and other trees shading the way. This is very much like the type of vegetation you would find in the Sierra Nevada. The leaf-littered trail starts up gradually, and you will see a lot of fallen trees along the way. The trail takes stepping stones across rivulets, then rounds a corner to take you into a patch of sun with a view of the trees on the adjacent mountainside. In the sunny parts, you might be surprised by some delicate wildflowers near the trail. Then once again you are led into the shade of the forest. The ascent is gentle in places, steeper in others. At times the

Along Observatory Trail.

trail becomes narrow and rocky. A nimble-footed trail dog will have no trouble here, but keep him with you, on the leash.

Part of the way up there is a bench to rest and look out over the Mendenhall Valley. There are ravines to cross before you reach the top, and in the spring these ravines may have streams rushing through. Before you reach the top, you will get a view of the white dome of the Palomar Observatory. At the top, you emerge onto the road that leads into the observatory.

Inaja Memorial Trail
Backcountry

Trail

Easy To Moderate

The Inaja Memorial Trail, near Julian, was dedicated in 1957 to honor eleven firefighters, two Forest Service employees, and nine workers from the Viejas Honor Camp who died fighting a 43,000-acre fire in this area in 1956. Inaja has a picnic area, in addition to the trail. This is in the Palomar Ranger District.

Directions

Highway 79, from the north, and Highway 78, from the west, join at the town of Santa Ysabel. Together, they proceed eastward up the mountain toward Julian. About a mile along the road from Santa Ysabel, there is a sign and a driveway on the right for Inaja Memorial Trail. Turn in and you will find a small parking lot.

Description

Near the parking lot, there is a memorial plaque to honor those who died in the fire nearly 50 years ago. A few picnic tables are scattered here and there among the large oak trees.

The trail begins just beyond the restrooms. Material on the Cleveland National Forest web site indicates that it is a loop trail of half a mile. Another source lists it as a one-mile loop. At any rate, it is not very long, but it did seem longer than half a mile to me.

It starts up gently, an easy hike at first. The dirt trail does a switch back to a slightly higher level. There are large granite rocks, including one impressive granite tower at the first turn in the trail. Manzanita, sage, wild lilac, and other chaparral-type plants line the trail, along with dry grasses. Live oaks are abundant on the nearby hillsides.

Part of the way up the view suddenly opens up and you see the far reaches of the Santa Ysabel Valley spreading out below you. It was named by the Spanish padre Father Juan Mariner when he came through the area in 1795. He chose the valley for locating a sub-mission, or *asistencia*, a few years later. Mission Santa Ysabel still stands, although it is not the original building.

Forcing yourself away from the view, you continue up the path and around, and finally reach the top, where you will find a stone platform with an overlook and a directional marker, pointing in the direction of the San Diego River Valley and neighboring mountain peaks.

View from Inaja Memorial Trail.

Downhill the trail stops being easy. It is steeper down than up, and our feet slid on fine gravel in some sections of the downhill trail. Still the steeper parts were intermittent. The looping trail eventually comes back to the place where we started. Getting down the steeper sections might be difficult with some dogs. Others will take it with ease. But hang on to that leash.

Lightning Ridge Trail
Backcountry

The Lightning Ridge Trail, in the Laguna Mountains, provides a fairly easy hike from the Laguna Campground to the top of a ridge with broad and beautiful views. The trail is a 1.3-mile loop. This is an excellent hike for you and your dog.

The Laguna Mountains are in the Descanso Ranger District of Cleveland National Forest. These pine-covered mountains form the western edge of much of the Anza-Borrego Desert.

Directions

From San Diego, take Interstate 8 east to Sunrise Highway (County Highway S-1). Go north on Sunrise Highway to the Laguna Campground, on the left. When you enter the campground, follow the road to the left to the amphitheater area. You can find parking near the amphitheater.

From the Julian area, you can take Highway 79 south, then turn left onto Sunrise Highway. Laguna Campground will then be on the right.

Description

Near the amphitheater, you will find a large stonework pedestal with a sign for the Lightning Ridge Trail. The narrow dirt trail takes off from the grassy picnic area to the ridge ahead. Soon you are on a gentle upward slope, surrounded by pines and oaks. As you rise, you see a narrow, grassy valley disappearing below. Another pine-covered ridge rises across the valley.

The trail does some switchbacks to gain elevation, but always gently. The path is rocky in places, but not difficult to travel. With rains more heavy than usual this year, there is a lot of green undergrowth, including small ferns, grasses, and some delicate wildflowers. Your dog will love the rich smells of pine forest and the many different plant species. We encountered a couple of

Along the Lightning Ridge Trail.

spots where trees had been cut up and woodchips were strewn around. We nearly lost the dirt trail there, but found it again and continued on.

At one point, the trail crosses a dirt utility road. We continued up our original trail to the top and discovered a dome-covered water tank, the Chula Vista Reservoir. Looking out from near the reservoir, you can catch a glimpse of the desert in the distant east. In the other direction, you overlook the campgrounds and Laguna Meadows, which was vividly green, again thanks to the recent rains.

We decided to take the dirt road down part of the way, but it was extremely rocky and uneven, and difficult to walk. So when we reached the intersection with the trail we had taken up, we opted to take it down as well.

Some hikers approach the Lightning Ridge Trail from the Sunrise Highway at the entrance to Horse Heaven Group Camp. We noticed a sign along the way pointing to the Horse Heaven Trail from Lightning Ridge Trail.

Desert View Nature Trail begins in the trees near Mount Laguna.

Desert View Nature Trail
Backcountry

The Desert View Nature Trail, for much of its distance, follows the extreme eastern edge of the Laguna Mountains, bordering on Anza-Borrego Desert State Park. This 1.2-mile looping trail starts in the Burnt Rancheria Campground. The trail is high in the mountains, at around 6,000 feet.

Directions

From San Diego, take Interstate 8 east to Sunrise Highway (S-1). Go north on Sunrise Highway to the Burnt Rancheria Campground, on the right. When you enter the campground, follow the left fork in the road about a one-quarter of a mile. You can find parking near the start of the Desert View Nature Trail.

From the Julian area, you can take Highway 79 south, then turn left onto Sunrise Highway. Burnt Rancheria Campground will then be on the left, past the Mount Laguna Store and the Laguna Mountain visitor center. (Note: The visitor center, with maps, information, and Adventure Passes for sale, is supposed to be open Friday through Sunday from May through September. However, since it is run by volunteers, it may not always be staffed during the scheduled hours.)

Description

A marker indicates where the Desert View Trail begins, just off of the small parking lot. It starts as a narrow dirt trail that heads straight through a broad picnic area, grassy, with scattered oak trees. The path then leaves the picnickers behind, veers left, and about a third of a mile along, this trail joins the Pacific Crest Trail that goes from Mexico to Canada. (See "More Ambitious Backcountry Hikes" at the end of this chapter for more details.) The two trails continue on together for a while.

Soon you are walking northward along the side of the mountain, heading gradually upward, though with only about a 50-foot gain in elevation over the course of the trail. The path is wide enough to stay on easily, but the land, covered with dry grasses and chaparral here, drops away sharply to the right just a few feet from the trail. You can see clearly to a mountainside across the way, covered in pine forest.

The trail leaves the mountain's edge and levels off through a woodland, with open sunny areas, then trees and undergrowth. An unexpected stone water fountain offers a drink in what seems like a wilderness. Continuing on, you soon reach a viewpoint looking eastward over the Anza-Borrego Desert far below. Soon after this, the two trails part, the Pacific Crest Trail continuing northward along the rim of the mountain, the Desert View Nature Trail turning west back into the woods.

It is an easy and pleasant walk in the woods back to the campgrounds area. The trail leaves you at the paved road in one of the loops of the Burnt Rancheria Campground. There may be paths leading through the campgrounds to the trailhead. We walked along the road the rest of the way back.

Anza-Borrego vista from the Desert View Nature Trail.

Wooded Hill Nature Trail
Backcountry

Trail

Easy To Moderate

Wooded Hill Trail, in the southern part of the Laguna Mountain Recreation Area, travels up to the 6,223-foot peak of Laguna Mountain and back to the start in a 1.5-mile loop. The elevation gain is only about 200 feet, since it starts at around 6,000 feet. There is also a half-mile loop that does not go all the way to the top.

Directions

From San Diego, take Interstate 8 east to Sunrise Highway (County Highway S-1). Go north on Sunrise Highway to Wooded Hill Road and turn left. Across from the sign for the Wooded Hills Trailer Circle, look to the left. There is a parking area and the trailhead for Wooded Hill Trail.

From the Julian area, you can take Highway 79 south, then turn left onto Sunrise Highway. The turn onto Wooded Hill Road will then be on the right.

Vista from the Wooded Hill Trail.

Description

The dirt path takes off from the trailhead across a level area at first, through high grasses and past ancient fallen tree trunks. Soon you are into the wooded hill, filled with tall pine trees and abundant undergrowth. The trail rises gradually, switchbacks taking you to the next level. The path becomes somewhat rocky; sometimes the rocks provide a step up to the next level. Deep in the woods and on the east side of the peak, it was shady in the afternoon, with shafts of light entering here and there.

After a short distance, a trail marker directs hikers to take one path if they want the half-mile loop; the other path continues up for the 1.5-mile loop. I had planned to take the shorter loop, but being so close to the top, I decided to go on.

The Forest Service rates this hike as easy. I am calling it easy to moderate, because of the climb. It is not difficult, but it did take some effort.

Near the top, boulders crowd in with the pine trees. In one spot, the path goes between two boulders. When the trail leaves the trees, the view opens up for miles and miles, with mountains layered on mountains to the horizon. Some days you can see San Diego and even the Pacific Ocean from here.

Downhill through the woods is an easy trek, although the path gets narrow at times. Even when it is narrow, it is a well- established trail and you are not likely to lose it. Any dog who likes woodsy hikes will like this one. There will be plenty of deep pine scents and other wonderful smells. And with only 200 feet elevation gain, it will not be overtaxing to a pooch who has had some conditioning.

More Ambitious Backcountry Hikes

The Dripping Springs Trail is in the Agua Tibia Wilderness area of the Cleveland National Forest, which is in the Palomar Ranger District. It is approached from the north, in Riverside County, from the Dripping Springs Campground. The hike takes you 6.8 miles southward, back into San Diego County and up the mountain. The Forest Service rates this a strenuous trail. Along the way you are rewarded with views of distant peaks and valleys. At the top, you can either turn back and hike down, or continue on the Magee-Palomar Trail. To check on trail conditions before you go, call the Palomar Ranger's office at (760) 788-0250.

The Noble Canyon Recreation Trail is a 10.5-mile hike off the Sunrise Highway. This is also rated as strenuous by the Forest Service; it rises 1,680 feet. To start from the upper end, take Interstate 8 to the Sunrise Highway. About 13.5 miles up the highway, past the second cattle guard, there are two turnouts. You can park there. The trail starts from the west side. There are views as far as San Gorgonio from the heights of this trail. This is also a mountain bike and equestrian trail, so you might have company on the way. Warning: don't drink the water in the creek. To check on conditions, call the Descanso Ranger's office at (619) 445-6235.

The Pacific Crest Trail travels 2,650 miles, from the Mexican border near Campo to the Canadian border, through the three western states. This trail runs the gamut in term of difficulty. Several sections of it go through the Cleveland National Forest. Between the Descanso and Palomar portions of the national forest, the Pacific Crest Trail dips down into Anza-Borrego Desert State Park. Since in a state park you can only take dogs on roads (paved or unpaved), not on hiking trails, don't plan to walk from border to border with your dog. The Pacific Crest Trail then continues on northward, back to another section of Cleveland National Forest, so dogs are allowed there. The Cleveland National Forest web site has details of the parts of this trail that are within its borders. For complete information, go to the web site of the Pacific Crest Trail at *www.fs.fed.us/pct/*.

Taking flight at Lake Cuyamaca.

4 California State Parks

Introduction to California State Parks

There are two wilderness state parks located excluively in the mountains of San Diego County: Palomar Mountain and Cuyamaca Rancho. California state parks have rules that restrict where you can take your dog within their boundaries. While dogs are allowed on nearly all trails in the Cleveland National Forest, they are not permitted on most trails in the two adjacent state parks.

In state parks dogs are allowed only in campgrounds, picnic areas, parking lots, and a few other areas specifically designated as dog friendly. Your dog must be kept on a six-foot leash at all times while in the park. For the most part, they are not allowed on trails. The California State Parks web site lists the reasons:

• To protect the park's resources. Dogs, and their lingering scent, can frighten natural wildlife in the area. Dogs might carry diseases or parasites that could be transmitted to the local ani-

On the trail at Palomar Mountain State Park.

mals. And if they get loose, dogs can bother or even kill park wildlife.

• For the safety and enjoyment of other visitors. A dog's presence may scare other animals into hiding, reducing the number of wild animals that other hikers will be able to see. In addition, dog owners who don't clean up after their pets leave unwelcome deposits that are a nuisance to other visitors and may contaminate the local water supply.

• To prevent problems for you and your dog. Dogs wandering along trails may be bitten by snakes, raccoons, coyotes, or other wildlife they encounter. Dogs may also pick up ticks, thorns, or poison oak.

This being said, there are a few places within the local state parks where you can hike with your pet. Dogs are not allowed on the hiking trails, but there are some specified paved and unpaved roads within the parks where you can take your dog, on leash.

Palomar Mountain State Park
Backcountry

Trail
Easy To
Moderate

Palomar Mountain State Park covers 1,683 acres on Palomar Mountain, surrounded by Cleveland National Forest. The world-famous Palomar Observatory with its 200-inch Hale telescope is just a few miles from this park. The state park has camping and picnic facilities deep in pine and cedar forest at about 5,000 feet. There are hiking trails through the woods and across the meadows, but your dog is not allowed on these. Myers Fire Road is the one place in this park where you can hike with your dog.

Directions

Palomar Mountain State Park is northeast of the City of Escondido and due east of Fallbrook. From Interstate 15, take Highway 76 eastward, on the section called Pala Road, named after the Pala Indian Reservation. Follow this road through Pauma Valley with the impressive mountains of Cleveland National Forest on your left. About 20 miles east of Interstate 15, turn left onto County Highway S-6. You will begin to ascend, leaving behind the valley and the familiar hillside chaparral. Now you are on some real mountain roads, twisting and turning up to an elevation

Myers Fire Road

Paso Picacho Campground in Cuyamaca Rancho State Park.

of more than 5,000 feet. When you reach the intersection with County Highway S-7, you turn left. Palomar Mountain State Park is in three miles.

Description

Palomar Mountain is one of the few areas in southern California with a Sierra Nevada-like environment. You are surrounded by forest, with tall pines, spruce, and cedar. At the entrance to the state park, stop to pay $4 for parking if you are there to hike for the day. If you are planning to camp in one of the several campgrounds, you should call ahead for reservations. You can reserve a spot up to seven months before your planned trip, and you may pay by credit card.

Dogs are allowed on leash in campgrounds, picnic areas, and parking lots, and there are numerous campgrounds within the park. In Palomar Mountain State Park, there is one trail that you can hike with your dog — Myers Fire Road. This is adjacent to campsite 9 in the Doane Valley Campground area.

Myers Fire Road is an old dirt road, bordered by large trees and undergrowth. Through the two-mile course of the hike, there is an elevation gain of about 400 feet. On sunny days, the sun's rays slant through the trees and dappled shade covers the path in places. The lush forest fragrances give you and your fuzzy friend plenty of olfactory enjoyment.

As always in state parks, keep your dog on a leash no longer than six feet, and keep an eye on your surroundings. You may see mule deer near the fire road, and perhaps even coyotes or bobcats. As mentioned before, mountain lion sightings are rare, but possible. If you see a lion, report it to park authorities.

It gets hot up here in the mountains on summer days, so bring water for yourself and your pooch. If you are camping overnight, be aware that nights at this elevation can be cold, even in the summer. Pack and dress accordingly.

Cuyamaca Rancho State Park

Cuyamaca Rancho State Park was badly burned during the fires of October 2003. The park was closed for a while and a great deal of effort was required to clean it up, remove debris, and make sure the trails were safe. Park staff and teams of volunteers worked hard to get the park open again, and at this date, much of the park has been reopened.

The Paso Picacho Campground is large and rather spread out, so there is a lot of campground area, with roads, where you and your dog can walk. In addition to campground and picnic areas, there are three places in and around Cuyamaca Rancho State Park where you can actually take a hike with your dog. When you are within the park with your dog, you must stay on paved roads, always have him on a six-foot leash, and take plastic bags for cleanups.

Cuyamaca Peak Fire Road
Backcountry

The Cuyamaca Peak Fire Road, also called the Lookout Fire Road, starts in the Paso Picacho Campground area. From this fire road, you see the sad remains of many burned trees along the way. But if you make it to the top at Cuyamaca Peak, the view is spectacular.

Directions
If you take Highway 79 south from Julian, the entrance to Paso Picacho is about nine miles down the winding highway. The entrance to the campground is on the right. From Interstate 8, take the Descanso exit. After you turn onto Highway 79, Paso Picacho is about 8 miles north. You pay $6 per vehicle for the day rate.

Once inside the gate, park your car in the day parking area to the right and walk across to the road at the left of the entrance, where you will see a sign for authorized vehicles only. Walk in and pass the work vehicle area. You will find the Lookout Fire Road just past this, to the right.

There are still scars from the 2003 fires along the Cuyamaca Peak Fire Road.

Description

This is still a working, paved fire road. As you head up the road, you will be struck by the sight of black skeletons of charred trees, so many of them still standing. There is new undergrowth along the road, but it will be a long time before this part of the mountain looks like forest again. Yet other parts of the Paso Picacho Campground area still have beautiful old trees that survived the fires.

If you turn around as you go up the fire road you'll see the view behind has opened up to allow you to see Stonewall Peak, standing at 5,730 feet. At that point you cannot even see Cuyamaca Peak, where you are headed.

It is a 2.6-mile hike to Cuyamaca Peak, which rises to 6,512 feet, amounting to a gain of 1,642 feet on this road. The information from the state park calls this trail moderately difficult. Believe it. This is a long way up. Be sure to take along plenty of water for yourself and your dog. You are on an open road, with no shade, so it can get hot.

If you continue all the way to the top, and if the weather is clear, the view from Cuyamaca Peak extends from the Pacific Ocean on the west to the Salton Sea on the east.

Stonewall Mine Road
Backcountry

Trail

Easy To Moderate

This road leads through a high meadow to the Stonewall Mine section of Cuyamaca Rancho State Park. The paved road has two branches, one that leads to the Stonewall Mine entrance and one that turns toward the Los Caballos Horse Camp.

Directions

The Stonewall Mine Road intersects with Highway 79 south of Lake Cuyamaca and just about a mile north of the entrance to Paso Picacho Campground. (See Directions for Cuyamaca Peak Fire Road.) There is no place to park at the intersection with Highway 79, so you need to drive up to the entrance to the Stonewall Mine and park your vehicle. Then you and your dog can walk back, along the paved road.

Description

While you cannot take your dog into the Stonewall Mine area of the state park because there are only dirt trails, this paved road leading to it offers a good choice for about a three-mile

Trail to the Stonewall Mine.

Stonewall Mine

Gold was discovered at this site by William Skidmore in March of 1870. He named his mine the Stonewall Jackson Mine, in honor of the Confederate general. This was, for a while, the richest mine in southern California.

The town of Julian had developed because of the number of active mines in this area at the time, and the town of Cuyamaca was established right next to this mine, south of Lake Cuyamaca. During its peak production years, 1886 to 1891, some 200 men worked in the Stonewall Jackson Mine. But luck changed. The mine closed and the main 630-foot mine shaft was sealed in 1892.

hike. From the parking area, you start by walking down the hill you just drove up. It is not steep, but it will give you an uphill rise to tackle when you are coming back. There are many pine trees here that survived the fires and are doing well. The area opens up into a meadow, where you will find a fork in the road. You can choose between taking the road you drove in on, which is now to the right, or turning left and heading toward the Los Caballos Horse Camp. The horse camp road is probably less frequented, but either one gives you a pleasant walk near pine trees and past open grassy meadows. Both roads cross small bridges over the Little Stonewall Creek.

As always, be sure to bring water for yourself and your dog. This walk is not difficult, but it can get hot. Also remember your hat and sunblock. While there are some trees near the road, much of the way is in open sun. Watch for how your pet is walking, to see if he has a normal gait. His footpads might become tender on what could be hot asphalt. If necessary, find a shady spot or take him off the asphalt to give him a little relief.

These roads do not connect or loop, so you need to retrace your path to get back up to your car.

Lake Cuyamaca and Fletcher Island
Backcountry

Nearby Lake Cuyamaca is not actually in the Cuyamaca Rancho State Park. It is a separate recreational facility, operated by the Lake Cuyamaca Recreation and Park District and owned by the Helix Water District. I have included it here, since it is so close to the state park and it does allow dogs on leashes on all of its trails.

Directions

From Julian, take Highway 79 south about 6 miles. Or, from Interstate 8, take the Descanso exit, then Highway 79 north about

11 miles. The lake and the entrance are on the east side of the highway. The entrance is near the Lake Cuyamaca Restaurant and Store. There is a fee of $6 per day per car for picnicking and hiking. They also have camping and fishing.

Description

This lovely 110-acre lake is one of the few in San Diego county that is high in the mountains (4,620 feet) and surrounded by a pine forest. Unlike the nearby Cuyamaca Peak area, the trees around Lake Cuyamaca were not burned during the fires in 2003. The pine trees around the lake and on Fletcher Island are in their natural state.

This is a popular fishing lake and it is stocked regularly with a variety of types of fish. What is relevant here is that dogs are welcome anywhere around the lake, except in the water. You must have your dog on a leash at all times, but you can hike the trails with him, cross over to the island with him, even take him in a boat. Just don't let him jump in the water.

Trails go around the lake most of the year, although, since this is a reservoir, the margins of the lake change. There is also territory to explore on Fletcher Island. There are two ways to get onto the island. If you follow a trail around the southern

Lake Cuyamaca.

part of the lake, a bridge takes you across. The fences you will notice here separate the lake's recreational area from the Stonewall Mine area of Cuyamaca Rancho State Park. This trail along the lake may deteriorate with the changes in water levels. The easier way to get to Fletcher Island is to go to Chambers Park, north of the restaurant area, at the northwestern part of the lake. Chambers Park is available for camping and day use. There is a dike that allows you to walk across to Fletcher Island. Once on the island, you can wander around among the cedars and pines with your pet (still on leash, of course).

For more information on Palomar Mountain State Park, call (760) 742-3462. For more information on Cuyamaca Rancho State Park, call (760) 765-0755. For camping reservations at any California state park, call (800) 444-7275 or visit the web site at *www.parks.ca.gov.*

Bailey takes the author for a walk in Anza-Borrego Desert State Park.

Part Three: Desert Dogs
Anza-Borrego Desert State Park

Anza-Borrego Desert State Park, in the eastern one-fifth of San Diego County, is the largest state park in the 48 contiguous states. It covers some 650,000 acres that stretch about 60 miles north to south. I was unfamiliar with this vast area before I set out to take Bailey on desert hikes. I had no feel for the desert; I only connected it with extreme heat. People had told me about the beauty of the desert and the bountiful, unexpected life that you will find, particularly in the spring, but I never felt drawn to its landscape. I needed to discover its beauty, with Bailey's help.

I hoped that Bailey would be a cooperative companion here, and in this case, he was. It helped that we never met any other animals on our hikes, at least, not close up. He turned out to be a happy desert dog. And with him, we discovered the varied faces of this desert.

The Rules

Since this is a California state park, the same rules apply as in the state's other parks. Dogs are allowed only in designated areas, and must always be on a leash no longer than six feet. If you are camping, your dog should be kept inside a tent or vehicle at night. Canine park visitors must have and wear their licenses and be up to date with their shots.

As is always the case, whether you are in a campground or out on a remote desert road, you need to be certain that your dog will behave well. Even on a leash, vicious or noisy dogs are not welcome. And again, leave only paw prints. Pack plastic bags for cleaning up after your pet.

Leashed dogs are permitted on any road — paved or unpaved — in the Anza-Borrego Desert State Park, opening up about 500 miles of roads for exploration. Many of the roads are suitable only for four-wheel drive vehicles, but as long as they are roads, you and your dog can hike them together. Note: Do not take your dog on hiking trails or across unbroken desert terrain.

Be aware that the condition of unpaved roads in the desert can change. Sands shift with wind and rain. Dirt can get washed out, rutted, and uneven. What is drivable in a standard passenger vehicle one day may be suitable only for four-wheel drive vehicles a week later.

Desert Warnings

The desert is, by definition, hot. Midday temperatures in summer frequently exceed 100 degrees Fahrenheit and can rise up more than 120 degrees. Parts of the park may be closed from June to September; most people visit between September and June, and even then, heat can be excessive. When you do plan a hike in the desert, it is best to go in the early morning hours, before 10 a.m., or late afternoon and early evening, well before sundown.

Always take water with you on your hike. Carry enough for yourself and your dog. Bailey will sometimes drink from the stream of a tipped bottle, but we take a plastic bowl in the backpack. He laps up a surprising amount after a walk, even if the day does not seem extremely hot.

One advantage of the strict rules about walking your dog only on a short leash and only on roads is that it gives you more

Borrego Palm Canyon Campground.

control in protecting your pet. Many roads, both paved and unpaved, have cholla cactus or other prickly plants in sandy encroachments into the road. Be sure to keep your curious dog away from these desert plants. Cactus thorns in the fur are something you want to avoid. It is a good idea to pack tweezers in your first aid kit, just in case.

A short leash will also help you keep your dog away from any rattlesnakes or other desert wildlife that you might encounter. A rattlesnake bite can kill a dog. You don't want your pet to be hurt, and you cannot allow him to chase or harass the animals that live there. Bailey took an interest in a couple of toads we encountered, but we held him back, and all three of us watched as they hopped past. Staying on a road allows you to see the path ahead and to the sides, at least the width of a car. Be alert.

Visitor Center

The Anza-Borrego Desert State Park Visitor Center was built underground, so that it does not intrude on the desert landscape.

It is located just west of the town of Borrego Springs, at the end of Palm Canyon Drive. Signs direct you to parking and to the visitor center itself.

This 7,000-square-foot facility features exhibits, maps, books, and a helpful staff happy to answer your questions. New exhibits were installed in 2005, showing the geologic history of the desert and displays of fossils found here. There is also a diorama of the wildlife living in Coyote Canyon. The visitor center is a good place to start a visit to the area.

The center is open daily from October through May, from 9 a.m. to 5 p.m. In the summer, June through September, it is only open on weekends and holidays.

For more information, call the visitor center at (760) 767-4205, visit *www.anzaborrego.statepark.org/* or the California State Parks web site at *www.parks.ca.gov.*

Dog Hikes

With more than 500 miles of roads, this book offers merely a sampling of the many places where you and your dog can hike. I have clustered the discussions around the major highways that cross the park.

Get maps at the visitor center before you start. If you plan to drive part of the way on the unpaved roads, be sure you have a shovel in your vehicle. If the road gets too sandy or difficult to drive, pull over in a pull-off area (there are many on most of these roads), park your vehicle, and start your hike.

Wear a hat and douse yourself in sunblock. Then grab your water, your dog's leash, and take off.

Bailey heads out Thimble Trail.

5 Anza-Borrego Desert State Park County Highway S-22

County Highway S-22 descends from the San Ysidro Mountains in the west, down the Montezuma Grade, with a dramatic view of the vast desert ahead. The road takes you into the town of Borrego Springs, the oasis within the state park. Highway S-22 meanders through the town, takes a turn around Christmas Circle, then continues eastward, re-entering the park in the northeastern section. There are many unpaved roads that take off from this highway. This northern section of the park along S-22 goes from palm-studded canyons in the west to deep-slashed badlands in the east.

Borrego Palm Canyon Campgrounds
Backcountry

Just west of the town of Borrego Springs and not far from the park's visitor center is the Borrego Palm Canyon Campground, a large, developed campground with 52 sites and hookups for RVs. There are restrooms, showers, potable water, and fire rings.

Picnic shelter in Borrego Palm Canyon.

Directions

Take County Highway S-22 west out of the town of Borrego Springs. Turn north on Palm Canyon Drive. Signs indicate where to turn left for the entrance to the campground.

Description

This sprawling picnic and campground is spread over a broad area, connected by paved roads looping around to different camping and picnic spots and RV hookups. Some of the picnic tables have stone shelters built by the Civilian Conservation Corps in the 1930s. The roads around the campground offer more than a mile of easy walking with your dog. You can stop and have a picnic in the shade, and enjoy the view of the nearby San Ysidro Mountains and get a close-up look at the desert vegetation.

There is a noted hiking trail from here to an oasis some miles up into the canyon, but you cannot take the trail with your dog. Walking the paved roads here is a good way to start getting acquainted with the Anza-Borrego Desert. Morning is a good time

Borrego Palm Canyon Picnic and Campground Rates

- **Day Use:** $6; seniors $5.
- **Camping Fees:** Hookup $24 a night; seniors $22; disabled $12.
- Self-registration at entrance.

for this walk. By afternoon, the pavement on the road may be too hot for your dog's paws, so be alert for this.

Coyote Canyon
Backcountry

This is a long canyon that the extends northwest for many miles between the San Ysidro Mountains on the west and Coyote Mountain to the east.

Directions

You enter Coyote Canyon at the north end of San Giorgio Road, just north of the town of Borrego Springs.

Description

The road into Coyote Canyon is rough and rocky in some places, sandy in others. As you are leaving town, the road parallels thick groves of grapefruit trees, unexpected in this desert clime. This is a significant crop for the town of Borrego Springs. The canyon is closed during the summer months, June through September, so that the bighorn sheep can reach sources of water.

If you want to drive in some distance before starting your hike, you will need a four-wheel drive vehicle beyond Desert Gardens. Even the earlier sections of the road could give standard automobiles some problems. The road is gated at Middle Willows.

Trail through Coyote Canyon.

No vehicles are permitted beyond that point. Remember, where the road stops, your hike with your dog stops, but there is plenty of unpaved road before you get to that point.

This hike with your dog can be a bit challenging, especially if you go beyond Desert Gardens, which is about 3 miles in. Be sure you are both in shape before you try it. You will be rewarded with a richness of desert vegetation, palm trees in the canyon, and riparian areas alongside the Coyote Creek.

Henderson Canyon
Backcountry

Henderson Canyon, located between Borrego Palm Canyon and Coyote Canyon, takes off in a northwesterly direction from Borrego Springs. It is not nearly as long as its neighboring canyons and does not have the palm trees that can be found at Borrego Palm or Coyote canyons.

Henderson Canyon is up ahead.

Directions

From Borrego Springs, follow Henderson Canyon Road west, alongside the grapefruit groves. This leads to the head of the Henderson Canyon road. At the entrance on the right is a sign indicating a privately owned area called Galleta Meadows. Permission has been granted to the public for use.

Description

A sandy, gravel road extends about 5 miles into this canyon. There is plenty of room near the start to park your car off the road. The road becomes narrow and quite sandy, and cholla appears very near to the road in places. Be sure to keep your dog close as you walk past. Bailey likes to sniff anything he can reach, so I stay alert and keep him away from anything prickly. The hike starts out fairly flat, then becomes steep as you get further in. You might not want to subject your dog to the final steepest, roughest part of this hike. Galleta grasses, ocotillo, and sage, as well as the cholla, cover the surrounding terrain in the earlier parts of this walk.

Thimble Trail
Backcountry

Although it is called Thimble Trail, this is actually an unpaved road, heading southward from County Highway S-22 toward the Borrego Badlands.

Directions

From the town of Borrego Springs, go about four miles east along County Highway S-22. Thimble Trail takes off toward the south from the highway.

Description

It is a gravel road for some distance, somewhat rocky and sandy, but quite drivable. It would be best driven in a four-wheel drive vehicle. Dry grasses cover most of the hillside, with other low desert scrub. Hiking along the road for a while, we came across several anthills. Be sure to keep your dog out of these. The road is wide enough to avoid them if you are paying attention.

We saw other paw prints and tracks in the sand, but did not see any other wildlife. Thimble Trail goes over rises and down again, continuing for a little more than 2 miles. Then it meets Short Wash, which connects with both Palo Verde Wash to the east, and Font's Point to the west. The road continues in both directions, so you can keep on hiking either way.

From the intersection, if you walk a sort distance to the east, then turn south, and you can hike along a road that leads to Vista del Malpais for a broad view of the Borrego Badlands.

Other Roads off County Highway S-22

Font's Point and Inspiration Point, both west of Thimble Trail, are four-wheel drive roads. Font's Point, in particular, is very sandy and hard to drive. Hiking in with your dog is permitted, since they are roads. Both lead to points several miles in where you can overlook the Borrego Badlands.

On the north side of County Highway S-22 in this area, all roads descend very steeply into a chasm before continuing on, and are not very suitable for dog walking.

Bailey on the trail with the author at Plum Canyon.

6 Anza-Borrego Desert State Park Highway 78

Highway 78 comes east from Julian, down through
Banner, and crosses County Highway S-2 in the San
Felipe Creek area at Scissors Crossing. It then winds
through another rocky section, skirting the edge of the North
Pinyon Mountains, and enters the western edge of Anza-Borrego
Desert State Park. The highway then opens up to the Yaqui Flat,
and the broad desert beyond, with unpaved roads taking off to
the north and south.

Archaeologists have found numerous artifacts from the early
Indians who lived in and around Yaqui Flat. If you come across
an arrowhead or a shard of pottery, however, leave it in place.
These artifacts and all plants and rocks are protected. Highway
78 continues eastward through the state park to Ocotillo Wells
and out toward the Salton Sea.

Taking in the sights along the Grapevine Canyon trail.

Plum Canyon
Backcountry

Just down the grade as the desert opens up in front of you, vegetation clears a little on the right and you can see a park sign with a small, shingle visor over it. This is the entrance to Plum Canyon, which takes off southward and back toward the Pinyon Mountains.

Directions

Going eastward on Highway 78, right out of the mountains, down from Banner, you pass the junction with County Highway S-2 at Scissors Crossing. You are in Anza-Borrego Desert State Park now, but you need to continue on through some more winding turns through the North Pinyon Mountains. As soon as you see open desert spreading before you, look for the turnout and the sign on the right. There is easily room to pull off the highway and park your vehicle.

Description

The gravel road is broad and follows close to the rock-covered hillside for about 2 miles. (A hiking trail goes on from there, but not for dogs.) This is high desert and has some tall creosote, desert willow, and clumps of grasses. The road was very quiet and was our own private path on the late afternoon we visited. Bailey found plenty to sniff at, but nothing to bark at, fortunately. The desert wildlife are usually good at staying out of sight, which is good for them and good for us, given the sometimes loud proclivities of our pooch.

Grapevine Canyon
Backcountry

The Grapevine Canyon road begins near where the San Felipe Creek meets the Yaqui Flat, and continues in a northwesterly direction. The canyon itself goes on for many miles.

Directions

The entrance to the Grapevine Canyon road is well hidden amid grasses and creosote. We passed it twice before we actu-

Grapevine Canyon offers a beautiful vista.

Tamarisk Grove Campground

Tamarisk Grove is a popular campground, with shade trees around 27 campsites. It is on County Highway S-3, just north of the intersection with Highway 78. Tamarisk Grove has all the necessary facilities: drinking water, flush toilets, showers, sheltered picnic tables and barbecues, but no electrical hookups. It is a relatively compact camping area, and has only hiking trails immediately around it, trails where your dog is not allowed. You can have him in the campground, on a leash. At night he must be restrained in a vehicle or a tent.

From Tamarisk Grove, it is not far by car to Plum Canyon or Grapevine Canyon.

ally found it. It goes northward off Highway 78, just across from the entrance to Plum Canyon (see Plum Canyon directions).

Description

Once you get on the gravel road, it widens out and has some pullout areas where you can leave your car. The road runs alongside the wash, and you can see the cliffs across the way and the greener creosote and desert willow in the lower regions of the Yaqui Flat that receive more water. There is some scattered cholla on the higher land near the road. To the south and above Grapevine Canyon road is the rocky hillside where Highway 78 ascends west toward Julian. Grapevine Canyon road extends only a mile before it turns into a hiking trail. Then you and your dog need to turn back. It was a gorgeous, sunny-but-cool morning when we walked along Grapevine Canyon. I began to see and feel why it is that people love the desert.

Other Roads off Highway 78

Traveling eastward, there are several other unpaved roads off Highway 78 before you reach Borrego Springs Road, which takes you north into the town of Borrego Springs. Most of the roads take off toward the south.

Lizard Canyon and Mine Canyon are four-wheel drive roads, quite sandy and, at times, hard to spot from the highway. Keep in mind that with these sandy and rocky unpaved roads, sands move and vegetation encroaches. It is always a good idea to call or visit the visitor center to check on current conditions.

There is also a road out to Stag Cove, an RV campground.

Bailey takes a drink at the Bow Willow campground.

7 Anza-Borrego Desert State Park County Highway S-2

County Highway S-2 draws a roughly diagonal line from County Highway S-22 in the northwest to Interstate 8 in the southeast, parallel to the trend of the mountain ranges and major fault lines. This was the route of early Spanish expeditions across the desert in search of a passage from inland Mexico to the coast of California. Later it served as both a military corridor and an immigration route. By the mid-1800s the valleys crossed by S-2 were used by the horse-drawn stages of the Butterfield Overland Mail for transporting mail and passengers. There are several historic markers along the way, honoring some of those who passed this way, and indications of the stage stations where wayfarers rested.

County Highway S-2 south of SR-78 goes through Earthquake Valley, across a pass to Blair Valley, then over another pass to Vallecito Valley. It passes near the Carrizo Badlands, while continuing southeast and out of Anza-Borrego Desert State Park.

Headed up Pinyon Mountain Road.

Pinyon Mountain Road
Backcountry

Pinyon Mountain Road is in the high desert, in Earthquake Valley, starting at an elevation of about 2,200 feet. The long, unpaved road extends far into the Pinyon Mountains to the east.

Directions

Driving south from SR-78 on S-2, Pinyon Mountain Road comes in on the left about 6 miles past the site of the former San Felipe Stage Station.

Description

Pinyon Mountain Road is a fairly narrow gravel road leading off toward the mountains. The road gets sandy and rough; much of it is suitable only for four-wheel drive. A golden eagle swooped down just in front of our car as we were driving in here. The presence of lots of cholla near the road means that when you are walking with your dog, you need to keep a particularly close eye on him while you are enjoying the scenery. He will not know the cholla is prickly until it is too late.

This is quite a picturesque spot with the backdrop of mountains on both sides. If the light is right, the cholla seem to have halos around them, which become the thorns when you get close. There is a pullout area where you can leave your car. About a half mile from the highway, the road curves around a rocky outcrop and soon is ascending into the mountains. It continues for about 7 miles and goes through The Squeeze, a narrow passage between two rocks, and then comes to a steep drop-off. If you haven't turned around to head back by this time, do it now.

Blair Valley
Backcountry

Blair Valley, site of a dry lakebed, stands at 2,250 feet elevation, right next to the Pinyon Mountains. The valley has a good size campground looping around a large area, and a long unpaved road.

Directions

Continuing south on County Highway S-2, about 6 miles from SR-78, just over a small pass and around the bend from Pinyon Mountain Road, you will find the entrance to Blair Valley on the left.

Description

At the entrance to Blair Valley, the road begins looping in several directions around level grassy areas. A sign gives mileage to three destinations: Marshal South (at Yaquitepec on Ghost Mountain), 3.2 miles; Morteros, 3.7 miles; and Pictographs, 5.0

Dirt road winds through Blair Valley.

Blair Valley Road.

miles. These final destinations are all accessible only by hiking trails in the far reaches. Not for you and your dog. Still, there is plenty of good walking along the way for both of you.

The dirt road curves around, following the line of the rocky foothills on the east, with the grassy lakebed on the west, dotted with a few isolated trees. At one point the road splits and loops around again, paths criss-crossing. Bailey reveled in the open path here, pulling hard on his leash as if he knew where he wanted to go, delighting in the desert air. We did not meet any wildlife here, although we had seen a coyote crossing the road earlier. I hoped Bailey would not meet up with one, coming around a creosote bush, although the coyote would probably have the sense to take off when it saw humans.

The sudden appearance of a low-flying Navy combat plane, veering just above the hill, curving sharply to the left, and disappearing over the next hill was a bit jarring in the peaceful desert scene. With the strong presence of Navy and Marine Corps, that scene could happen anywhere in San Diego County.

Agave bloom in Oriflamme Canyon

Oriflamme Canyon
Backcountry

Oriflamme Canyon marks a pass through the Cuyamaca Mountains first known to be used by Spanish Presidio Captain Pedro Fages, traveling from San Diego to the desert in 1772. Two years later, another Spaniard, Juan Bautista de Anza, led his expedition across the desert some miles distant. In 1854, Oriflamme Canyon became the route for mail service between San Diego and Yuma.

Directions

Continuing south on County Highway S-2, past Blair Valley, is an historical landmark, acknowledging the Mormon Battalion's work in carving out a road here with only hand tools. Following through Box Canyon, just around the bend, look for a long gravel road to the right that leads toward the mountains. That is Oriflamme Canyon Road.

Description

When we first turned onto this narrow gravel road, I noticed that many 10- to 12-foot agave plants with yellow plumes of flowers stood proudly on both sides of the road. Aha, I thought. This is why it is Oriflamme Canyon — the golden flame-shaped plume

Heading into Mortero Wash.

of blossoms. However, after research to confirm this, I learned that the canyon was named after the Oriflamme gold mine in the area, which in turn was named after a ship that regularly steamed between San Francisco and San Diego in the heady days of the gold rush.

The road is rocky and becomes difficult going in anything but a four-wheel drive vehicle. I suggest you find a wide spot in which to park and take to foot and paw. The road is fairly level for quite a way before it starts up the mountain. This road goes out of the state park eventually. Watch for signs.

Bow Willow Canyon
Backcountry

Trail
●
Easy

Bow Willow Canyon has a popular campground at the site of an early Indian village. It has only 16 camp-sites, much smaller than the more developed Borrego Palm Canyon Campground, but Bow Willow Canyon does have restrooms, picnic tables shaded with ramadas, and drinking water. The campground is some distance off Highway S-2, so you can walk your dog all along the road to the campground.

Bow Willow Road.

Directions

The road to the Bow Willow Campground is off County Highway S-2, about 14 miles south of Vallecito Stage Station. The unpaved road takes off to the west.

Description

The road to Bow Willow Campground is very sandy, and a standard vehicle might get stuck. There are places to pull off to get out and walk, so we did early on. The campground is nearly two miles from the highway, and the area seems very remote. While walking along the sandy road, with the highway already out of sight, I felt down to my bones the silence of the desert. The only sounds were a buzzing insect in the flowers of a desert shrub and the slight, hollow sound of the breeze in my ear. Tall ocotillo, scattered cholla, and sage seemed to go forever. In the distance I could see a darker green of vegetation along the line of a creek. A section of road takes a short detour to the top of Egg Mountain, offering a grand view over the Carrizo Badlands to the east.

A hiking trail takes off from the campground, a rocky, looping path, but again, a path not for dogs. At this point you and your dog need to turn around at the campground and return to your vehicle, which, depending on where you parked, can make the walk nearly 4 miles.

Other Roads off County Highway S-2

South Carrizo Creek is a four-wheel drive road that heads east, just south of Bow Willow Canyon off County Highway S-2. This road continues eastward into the Carrizo Badlands, but don't go too far. At just over 5 miles in, it goes into what the U.S. Navy euphemistically calls the Carrizo Impact Area, meaning an area of live target practice. It is no longer used for that, but it is closed to the public, due to the presence of live bombs that are still found there.

Canyon Sin Nombre is well known for the rich geologic history revealed over the course of the canyon. The road calls for four-wheel drive, and begins with a rather steep descent. Several miles east, it joins Carrizo Creek.

Mortero Wash, some miles south of Canyon Sin Nombre and southwest off the highway, crosses Lava Flow Wash, reflecting volcanic activity in the area millions of years ago.

Two Goldens and a Lab enjoy a day at Live Oak Park in Fallbrook.

Part Four:
Nature Hikes in Town

Between the mountains and the sea, San Diego County is laced with canyons, mesas, hills and lagoons. This varied topography hosts a richness of vegetation and even now provides a refuge for native wildlife. While the county has succumbed to rapid development in recent decades, city and county leaders (often responding to community groups) have had the foresight to protect and preserve large areas as regional parks and open spaces.

The City of San Diego has set aside nearly 6,000 acres in the Mission Gorge area, south of Highway 52, as Mission Trails Regional Park. Mission Trails features a visitor and interpretive center, hiking trails at a variety of levels of difficulty, and the historic Old Mission Dam.

There are other protected open spaces with hiking trails, including Tecolote Canyon Natural Park, Los Peñasquitos Canyon Preserve, and San Dieguito River Park. The city also manages the San Pasqual–Clevenger Canyon Open Space Park, even though it is outside the city boundaries. At all City of San Diego parks and open spaces, dogs are allowed, but must be on a short leash, no longer than eight feet.

The county of San Diego has also preserved areas of open space, such as San Elijo Lagoon Ecological Reserve on the coast, Dos Picos Regional Park nestled in a rocky hillside, and Sycamore Canyon/Goodan Ranch Open Space Preserves in a long interior valley. At all county parks and open spaces, dogs must be on a leash no longer than six feet. Dogs are allowed on hiking trails in most county parks, but are not permitted in the following open space preserves: Agua Caliente, Quail Gardens, Volcan Mountain, and Santa Ysabel.

Other cities and districts in the county have also established areas of protected natural environment that people can enjoy with their pets. For example, Escondidio has the Daley Ranch, Olivenhain has the Elfin Forest Recreational Reserve, Carlsbad has a series of trails to explore the natural terrain still left within the city. And Santee Lakes, owned and operated by the Padre Dam Municipal Water District, has a designated dog hike area around the northernmost lakes.

These and other choice dog-friendly hiking spots are covered in the following chapters.

On a walk in Mission Trails Regional Park.

8 City of San Diego Regional Parks and Open Spaces

San Diego has some surprisingly large natural areas within its city limits. Residents can drive a short distance and find a regional park or an open space preserve heavy with chaparral, crossed with trails, some shaded by sycamore and live oak, with streams trickling through. Once you take off on a trail in these natural parks, you can easily forget that a housing development or a major highway is within sight of where you left your car.

All City of San Diego parks and open spaces allow you to take your dog with you, as along as you keep him on a leash of no more than eight feet in length. Having your dog on a short leash will enable you to keep him under control if there are other hikers or distractions on the trail. It also makes it easier for you to keep him out of poison oak and away from confrontations with snakes and other wildlife.

City rules require that your dog wear a current license on his collar and that he is up to date with his shots. You must pick up after your dog. The sign says, "Leave Only Paw Prints," and it means it, so be sure to bring plastic bags for cleanup.

Even with your dog on a leash, he must be socialized enough so that when you meet another hiker, another dog, or a mountain biker, he will not become aggressive.

San Pasqual–Clevenger Canyon Open Space Park
Backcountry

Trail

◻ ◆

Moderate To Strenuous

San Pasqual–Clevenger Canyon Open Space Park has a series of trails proceeding in opposite direction from two different starting points, south and north, on opposite sides of the highway. These trails are also part of the San Dieguito River Park Trails system. These trails offer some challenging hiking in the hills and canyons east of the San Pasqual Valley.

Directions

From Interstate 15, take the Via Rancho Parkway exit east. Turn right on San Pasqual Road. The signs will indicate you are heading toward the Wild Animal Park. There is another right turn at Highway 78, here called San Pasqual Valley Road. After passing the Wild Animal Park, the entrance to the southward trails at San Pasqual–Clevenger Canyon will be in just over 5 miles, on the right. The entrance to the northward trails at San Pasqual–Clevenger Canyon will be about a half mile farther on, and on the left (north) side of the highway.

Description

This is an area of steep canyons and sharply rising hills, covered with mixed chaparral vegetation. Chamise, black sage, laurel sumac and scrub oak line the hillside trails. Oak and sycamore shade the ravines.

From the south entrance to San Pasqual–Clevenger Canyon Open Space Park the trail starts to rise, gently at first, with occasional half-buried boards across the path providing a foothold. The dirt is a reddish loam and is rutted from the rains in parts of the trail. The path was narrow and overgrown in places when we were climbing, and I was glad I was wearing long pants and long sleeves to protect myself from scratches. The trail becomes steeper and turns frequently as it goes up the mountainside. If you stop to look around at the view, you realize how high

Clevenger Canyon vista.

you are above the highway and the canyon below. This is a nice hike if both you and your dog can handle some steep hills, both going up and coming down.

Just past the half-mile marker, there is a fork in the trail. The western trail goes yet higher and reaches an overlook of the San Pasqual Valley. The eastern trail from the fork descends into a ravine among towering oak and sycamore trees, and then climbs up the other side. This strenuous trail is a little over two miles long, one way.

The north trail that starts at the other entrance to the park, on the north side of the highway, descends steeply into the canyon, and continues on for ten miles. This is a strenuous hike. At this writing, this north trail is very overgrown, and at times the trail itself disappears. Before taking this trail very far, you should check with the park ranger office, at (858) 538-8082, to find out if the trail has been restored.

San Dieguito River Park, Bernardo Bay Natural Area
North County Inland

Trail

●

Easy

This section of the San Dieguito River watershed in the Rancho Bernardo area is called Bernardo Bay Natural Area and features the Piedras Pintadas Interpretive Trail. Bernardo Bay, a part of Lake Hodges, is a section of what will eventually be an open space preserve, the San Dieguito River Park, extending from the mouth of the San Dieguito River at Del Mar up the river, past Lake Hodges, all the way to Volcan Mountain, north of Julian.

Directions

From Interstate 15, take the West Bernardo Road exit and head west. As the road curves around southward, look to the right for the park sign that says Bernardo Bay Natural Area and the entrance to a dirt and woodchip parking lot. There is free parking.

Description

The Piedras Pintadas Interpretive Trail starts from the south end of the parking lot. You will find a kiosk with trail maps and other information. This trail is 3.8 miles round trip and takes you around the Bernardo Bay section of Lake Hodges. It is a fairly easy hike, although there is some elevation change — about 100 feet from the top to the water's edge. Piedras Pintadas has

Rocks tell a story along the Piedras Pintadas Interpretative Trail.

Bernardo Bay at Lake Hodges.

informative signs on large rocks along the route, several of them describing the lives and activities of the Kumeyaay Indians who lived in this area.

The wide trail leads gently downhill toward Lake Hodges. Deep rutting, developed during heavy rains, crosses parts of the trail. The surrounding terrain goes from dry grasses and rocky hillside at the start of the trail to the greens of riparian vegetation in some areas around Lake Hodges. As you near the lake, a bit of breeze coming off the water is refreshing to the face on a hot summer day.

You can walk with your dog on leash here, but be sure to stay on the trail. There are sensitive areas with protected plants and bird habitat. Here, in addition to the frequently spotted rabbits, squirrels and lizards, I caught sight of a raccoon scurrying off into the brush.

A juxtaposition of the urban and the natural environment is often found in San Diego County.

Lake Hodges

In 1916, Ed Fletcher convinced Santa Fe Railroad Vice President W.E. Hodges to finance the building of a dam near an existing small lake in the hills, to regulate stream flow and create a reliable water supply downstream. The railroad, being heavily invested in land in the San Dieguito area and needing water for irrigation, came up with the $350,000 needed for the project. This dam created Lake Hodges, a much larger lake. The dam and the lake were purchased by the City of San Diego in 1925.

Throughout the last century there have been periodic rumors of a lake monster in Lake Hodges. Searches were undertaken for Hodgee, as he was called, as he was called, and two photographs were captured, but no monster. No one knows if he is still in there, if he ever was.

As you walk along this trail toward the lake, you see a hillside on the right looking much as it did a hundred years ago; off to the left you see new houses on a ridge.

A footpath joining the trail at one point originates at the Rancho Bernardo Community Park just south of here, where you can find San Diego's newest off-leash dog park.

Los Peñasquitos Canyon Preserve
San Diego

Los Peñasquitos Canyon Preserve offers a mostly natural view of the county's hillside and canyon landscape in the northern part of the City of San Diego. It follows Peñasquitos Creek, with a shorter trail going alongside the creek's southern branch, known as Lopez Creek.

Directions

For the eastern entrance to Los Peñasquitos Canyon Preserve, take Mercy Road off Interstate 15. Continue westward to Black Mountain Road. The entrance to the park will be straight ahead.

For the western entrance, take Sorrento Valley Road off Interstate 805 and follow it eastward to the entrance.

Description

At either entrance to Los Peñasquitos Canyon Preserve you will find parking and restrooms. There is a $1 charge at the entry gate. The gates are open from 8 a.m. to 8 p.m. Dogs are allowed on leash only. This is a popular equestrian trail and bike path, so be sure your dog will be able to handle encounters of this kind. There are also warnings of encounters of a more serious kind. Coming off of the city streets as you enter the preserve, you might not expect warnings about mountain lions, but they have been spotted here, although rarely.

The main trail is about 6 miles long, with a small waterfall at about the three-mile mark. The trail, really a dirt fire road, starts from the east through a grassy meadow area, open and sunny, with a chaparral-covered hillside to the south, topped with houses.

We brought Bailey along on this hike, hoping that our attempts at training him were taking hold. This was a big test. He is great at walking on a leash if there are no distractions. He barked at the first horse that passed, and we apologized to the rider. We managed to keep him quiet as some bike riders wheeled by, but other dogs on the trail were, alas, his undoing. He barked loudly and pulled and squirmed, so we knew we had to get him off the trail.

If your dog gets along with people and animals on the trail, this is a very pleasant hike. It is mostly level, leading from the grassland into a riparian landscape at about the half-mile marker. The creek is close to the road there, and sycamore, live oak and an occasional palm tree, grow alongside the creek, shading the trail. A side trail takes off toward the north, leading to a small rustic bridge that crosses the creek. There are several bridges along the route. A group of equestrians splashed across the creek nearby while we were heading for the bridge.

On the north side, picking up a paved road you will find an old adobe ranch house from 1824. Free tours of the ranch house are given Saturday at 11 a.m. and Sunday at 1 p.m.

Tecolote Canyon Natural Park
San Diego

As a result of groups of citizens campaigning for the preservation of the canyon, the City of San Diego established this park in 1978. Planners made good use of the natural terrain in establishing Tecolote Canyon as a natural park, cutting across a long swath of the city, mostly out of view from the city streets. There are several points to enter this 900-acre park.

An easy trail at Tecolote Canyon.

Steeper trails are available at Tecolote Canyon.

Directions

The southern entrance to Tecolote Canyon Natural Park is at the nature center. From Interstate 5, take the Sea World Drive/ Tecolote Road exit east and follow Tecolote Road until it ends. There is free parking by the nature center.

At the northern end of the park, in Clairemont Mesa, take Clairemont Mesa Boulevard to Genessee Avenue. Turn south on Genessee, and then right on Bannock Street, and you will see the North Clairemont Recreation Center. Walk through the park southward, toward the canyon. You will find a trail and a sign for Tecolote Canyon.

There are trails that you can pick up off of Balboa and Genessee avenues, but there is no place to stop your car and park near these trailheads. You would need to walk in from the neighborhood.

Description

The nature center, on the southern end, has trail maps for Tecolote Canyon Natural Park. The San Diego Natural History Museum assisted the city in setting up this nature center as a small natural history museum of the area. It has helpful information and interesting exhibits about the plants, the animals, the area's faultlines, and the native Kumeyaay Indians who used to live here.

The trail takes off east and northward from the nature center. It is a dirt road in this part of the park, fairly level and a comfortable hike, with markers every half-mile. Tecolote Creek parallels the road here, and you can easily see the difference between the riparian vegetation, with its sycamores, live oak, and willow trees, and the chaparral and coastal sage on the opposite hillside.

The only animals I saw while hiking this trail were lizards, squirrels, birds, and butterflies, but park officials warn that, as with all of our San Diego canyons, there can be snakes, particularly rattlesnakes. On this wide dirt road it is easy to keep an eye out for such creatures and to keep your dog out of trouble. On some of the narrower trails, that is more difficult.

The trail that starts at North Clairemont Recreation Center descends steeply into the canyon and is a much narrower trail. Such is the case with the trails off Balboa and Genessee as well. Be sure that you and your dog are up to a more challenging hike before attempting these.

Mission Trails Regional Park
East County

Trail
●■◆
Easy To
Strenuous

Mission Trails Regional Park was established in 1974, and includes more than 40 miles of nature trails and nearly 6,000 acres of natural terrain. Its visitor and interpretive center is one of the best, with information on the native plants and animals, as well as displays depicting historic Kumeyaay Indian life in this area.

Directions

To get to Mission Trails Regional Park from the San Diego area or El Cajon, take Interstate 8 to the Mission Gorge Road/Fairmont Avenue exit. Proceed north about 4 miles, look for the large sign for the park at Father Junípero Serra Trail, and turn left. The entrance to the parking lot and the visitor center is a short distance in — a left turn just before you get to the pipe gate.

To get to the park from the north, take Highway 52 to the Mast Boulevard exit, turn left onto Mast, and then right onto West Hills Parkway. From there, turn right onto Mission Gorge Road, go about 2.4 miles, and turn right onto Father Junípero Serra Trail.

Walk crosses bridge at Mission Trails Regional Park.

Description

Wooden racks outside the visitor center hold trail maps with information on 25 recommended hikes. Each one shows the distance in miles, the elevation gain during the hike, and a category of difficulty, from easy and mostly level to very challenging for experienced hikers only.

The Visitor Center Loop Trail is a "level two" hike, okay for beginning dogs (and people) in good physical condition. It starts between Father Junípero Serra Trail and the visitor center, and begins a gradual decent on a dirt path, with sage and chaparral on both sides. You soon lose sight of the road and the buildings. The trail goes over a small wooden bridge as some trees and thick shrubs close in on the path. Then it opens up again into the sunshine. South Fortuna Mountain and Kwaay Paay Peak provide a mountainous background. Cactus and yucca intersperse with the chaparral along the path. The trail veers to the left and eventually parallels the San Diego River. We could hear the water rushing, but could not see it through the thick riparian growth.

After leaving the river, the trail takes off to the left again, this time uphill. The trail map indicates that this trail covers a 206 feet elevation gain, and I think it all happens right here. This is a broad section of trail, in open sun. You and your dog will be glad you brought water at this point. After the slope levels out again, a BMX bike path joins the trail, so it is advisable to keep your dog in close here. We met a couple of bikers, who just suddenly appeared from around a bend.

On the path at Mission Trails.

For more information on Mission Trails Regional Park, call (619) 668-3281 or visit the park's web site at *www.mtrp.org.*

For more information on parks, visit the City of San Diego Park and Recreation Department web site at *www.sandiego.gov/park-and-recreation.*

A walk at the Sycamore Canyon/Gooden Ranch Open Space Preserves.

9 County of San Diego Parks and Open Space Preserves

San Diego County has many parks and open space preserves that are available for a variety of recreational uses. There are picnic and hiking parks providing a bit of nature within the city environment, and there are wilderness parks in the chaparral-covered hillsides and in the pine-covered mountains. Dogs are allowed at most County parks and preserves on a leash of not more than six feet. Dogs are not permitted at all at the following open space preserves: Agua Caliente, Quail Gardens, Volcan Mountain and Santa Ysabel.

There has been some confusion in the past about whether dogs are allowed on hiking trails in San Diego County camping parks. The information on the County web site, using the legal language of the County ordinance, was unclear. This has been clarified: you may walk your dog on hiking trails in any County park, on a leash, except those parks mentioned above.

The ownership of some of the County parks and open space preserves is complicated by partnerships. For example, Blue Sky Ecological Reserve is a joint partnership of the California

Department of Fish and Game, the Department of Parks and Recreation of the City of Poway, and the County of San Diego. And Los Peñasquitos Canyon Preserve is listed as both a City of San Diego and a County preserve. I have designated one jurisdiction for each simply for the purpose of organization.

Guajome County Park
North County Coastal

Guajome County Park is a camping park on the eastern side of the City of Oceanside. It is an unexpected leafy green refuge just south of Highway 76. This is a good place for an easy walk around the park grounds by a lake, or a longer hike across the less developed part of the park.

Directions

Take Highway 76 to Guajome Lake Road, which is just east of North Santa Fe Avenue. Turn south onto Guajome Lake Road. The main park entrance is to the right. There is a $2 charge for day use parking. You pay at the entrance, and then put the receipt in your windshield.

Lake at Guajome Regional Park.

Description

This lovely 557-acre park has a small, spring-fed lake just south of Highway 76, populated by ducks and fish. The grassy hillside overlooking the lake, with occasional pine trees and graceful willows, provides room for play or for a picnic. A paved path leads around an area of picnic tables. On the Sunday afternoon I was there, a small black Lhasa Apso with a short summer haircut was resting near his people's picnic blanket (still on his leash) after a walk by the lake. Some people were fishing from the shore. Families were picnicking and children were playing on wood construction play equipment in a sandy area. There are picnic tables and barbecues on several levels, separated so that no one need to feel crowded.

Guajome is a camping park, with 34 campsites for tents or RVs, with electrical hookups, water, showers and rest rooms.

Lhasa Apso enjoys Guajome Park.

This park offers miles of natural hikes. One trail starts at the west end of the lake, goes southeastward alongside a marsh thick with cattails, then leaves the camping and picnic area to head across the large area of natural dry grasses and trees to the southeast corner of the park, about 3.25 miles away. There is also a trail that goes much of the way around the lake. Guajome can provide a good getaway right in the city. If your dog doesn't get along with ducks, it would be a good idea to keep him away from the lake. I would not trust Bailey to take kindly to ducks, so he did not get to go to this park.

At the southern end of the park and then across North Santa Fe Avenue lies an impressive ranch house, the Rancho Guajome Adobe, built in the 1850s that became a hub of social activities for residents of that era. It was owned by Ysidora Bandini and her husband, Army Lieutenant Cave Johnson Couts, who put on grand fiestas here. Docent tours of the ranch house can be arranged by phone (760-724-4082), but your dog will not be allowed on the tour.

San Elijo Lagoon Ecological Reserve
North County Coastal

The San Elijo Lagoon lies between Solana Beach and Encinitas, on both sides of Interstate 5. This broad wetland is rich in plants, fish, and showy birds like the Great Blue Herons and Snowy Egrets. There are more than 5 miles of trails around the lagoon.

Directions

The San Elijo Nature Center is at 2710 Manchester Avenue, on the Encinitas side. Take Interstate 5 to Manchester. Go west on Manchester, around the curve, and look for the sign on the left. One trail takes off from here.

There are several approaches for other trails around the lagoon. For one trailhead, take Interstate 5 to Lomas Santa Fe. Turn west, then continue down the hill to North Rios Avenue. Turn right (north) on North Rios and follow it to the end. Two trails take off from this spot.

Two other trailheads are accessed from Interstate 5 at Lomas Santa Fe, eastward. For one trailhead, turn left on Santa Helena Street and follow it around to the lagoon. For the other, turn left on Santa Helena as above, then turn left on Santa Victoria and left again on Santa Carina.

Description

I was surprised to learn that in this protected ecological reserve, dogs are allowed to visit — on leash, of course. Sensitive areas are marked with signs, so you and your dog need to stay on the main trails.

Changes in the Lagoon

In its natural state, a lagoon, like San Elijo, is an estuary where water from inland streams flows toward an outlet to the sea, and in turn, salt water from the tides flush the same area, maintaining a balance with a salt water-freshwater marsh environment. Birds, plants, and marine animals have developed a hardiness to survive as a part of this ecosystem.

Since Highway 101 and the railroad were built across the western edge of the lagoon in the early 1900s, and later, Interstate 5 was constructed to intersect the area, the natural flows have been altered. While channels under the highways allow water to flow, the patterns of flow and the patterns of sediment deposition from the streams have changed. Such changes affect the survival of plant and animal species in the lagoon.

San Elijo Lagoon.

A level dirt path leads from the nature center out into the lagoon, a few feet above water level. Illustrated signs are stationed along the path, with information about the lagoon and its fish, birds, and vegetation. The smells were rich and slightly pungent so near the marsh at the time of my visit, in early summer. This is an easy hike that loops around the northwest part of San Elijo Lagoon.

From North Rios Avenue on the south side of the lagoon, one trail takes off descending toward the east, parallel to the lagoon, and continues along to the Interstate, then branches off into two trails. It goes through an area of coastal sage scrub vegetation, with the lagoon off to the north.

The other trail from North Rios Avenue descends north and west, going around the bend to face the Pacific Ocean, visible just across Old Highway 101. The main dirt trail continues around, still above the lagoon, and curves around to the southwest end, near the railroad tracks, then turns north to parallel the highway.

I took a narrow dirt path branching off from this trail, which goes fairly steeply downhill toward the lagoon. It is so narrow that I scraped past waist-high coastal sage on the way down. The path levels and broadens out just a few feet above the level of the salt marsh. Here too, the air was thick with the fragrance of salt water and marsh plants. Even with the traffic sounds from

Bridge at Live Oak County Park.

Highway 101, there was a quiet stillness in the lagoon, punctuated by the croaking of frogs and the calls of birds.

Live Oak County Park
North County Inland

Live Oak County Park is a picnic park on the east side of Fallbrook, with tall oaks sheltering large picnic areas, tennis and volleyball courts, and children's play equipment. Dogs and dog owners are welcome here; dogs must be on leash.

Directions

From Highway 76, take the Gird Road exit north, passing the long and lovely Fallbrook Golf Course. When you reach the intersection with Reche Road, continue straight ahead to the entrance to the park. As you enter, you see a sign that says, Slow. The next sign says, Slower Please.

If you are approaching from Fallbrook Village, you can take Reche Road east and turn left into the park at the intersection with Gird Road.

Description

As with other San Diego County parks, there is a $2 charge for day parking. There is plenty of space for parking.

This 26-acre refuge has a large area for picnics and barbecues, all in the shade of the great old oak trees. That shade is very appealing on a hot summer afternoon. The creek running through the park goes through stone wall channels, forming a drainage system that creates small waterfalls in places. Bridges cross the channel in several different parts of the park.

Paths lead around and through the park from one area to another. It is mostly level, so it is an easy walk, but has enough distance to provide some exercise. I came across a man with three happy dogs, two Goldens and a yellow Lab, taking a vigorous afternoon walk. These beauties stopped to pose for a picture. They were shelter dogs and had obviously found a good home.

On one side of the parking lot is the entrance to a botanical garden with native plants and little gravel paths around the planted gardens. If you walk your dog in here, be sure to keep him off of the display plants.

Felicita County Park
North County Inland

Felicita County Park in Escondido is a picnic park for day use. This 53-acre park is very natural for the most part, with large oaks sheltering picnic tables by a creek. A children's play equipment area is near a grassy

Picnic spot at Felicita County Park.

spot just up from the restrooms. A ball field and a volleyball court lie off to one side.

Directions

Felicita can be approached from either Felicita Road or Via Rancho Parkway, off Interstate 15. I took Felicita Road, west, which takes a left turn when you get off the freeway. Follow Felicita Road south until you see the stone entrance to the park.

Description

The fee for day parking is $2. An automated pay station accepts dollar bills, and gives you a receipt to put on your dashboard. The road straight ahead leads you to a parking area and a welcoming oak-covered shady area. Felicita Creek runs through the park, with footbridges to cross it. Another road leads to a large expanse of park on the south.

You can hike with your dog on leash anywhere in the park here. Narrow dirt trails lead from one section of the park to another and all around the park. It was quiet on the weekday that I visited, with no dogs at all and few people. I was kept company by the birds and the squirrels. It is probably a lot busier on weekends. There are a couple of picnic areas that are available for large groups. (For groups larger than 50 people, reservations can be made through the San Diego County Parks and Recreation Office at 858-565-3600 or 877-565-3600).

Even with all of the picnicking and possible activity, about a third of the 53 acres of the park, the part east of the creek, is undeveloped, natural, open for wandering, quiet contemplation or a romp with your dog. It can provide a respite from city hustle and bustle and some exercise for you and your dog, without a long drive out of the city.

Blue Sky Ecological Reserve
North County Inland

The Blue Sky Ecological Reserve is 700 acres of natural southern California hillside and canyon on the western edge of Poway, extending from Espola Road on the west nearly to Lake Ramona. As mentioned above, it is managed by the California Department of Fish and Game, the County of San Diego, the City of Poway, and a non-profit organization called the Friends of Blue Sky Canyon. The name comes

On the trail at the Blue Sky Ecological Reserve.

from the 410-acre Blue Sky Ranch, which was purchased in 1989 to be part of the reserve.

Directions

From Interstate 15, take the Rancho Bernardo Road exit east. This becomes Espola Road as it enters the City of Poway. The entrance to Blue Sky Ecological Reserve is on the left, just past the point where the Espola Road turns southward.

Description

As you enter the road to the parking lot, turn right, and you will find free parking. In one of the seeming incongruities of a wild park within city limits, there is also a bus stop and bench for hikers arriving by Poway Transit. At the southern end of the parking lot, you pick up the Green Valley Truck Trail. Dogs are allowed here on leash only. Bicycles are not permitted.

The hills of Blue Sky Ecological Reserve are typical of the natural chaparral, sometimes called the "Elfin Forest." The wide dirt trail descends gently, curving around in and out of the deep shade of tree cover at times, then emerging again into the sun. In the oak woodlands that follow the creek, you will see the rare Engelmann oak, as well as the more common live oak.

There is a lot of poison oak growing here in the reserve, so you need to stay alert and keep your dog away from anything that looks suspicious. At any rate, both you and your dog must stay on the trail.

The Oak Grove and Creekside Trail takes off from the Green Valley Truck Trail to the left and goes down to the creek, but a sign indicates that no horses or dogs are allowed on this trail.

If you follow the Green Valley Truck Trail to the boundary of the reserve, you will be overlooking Lake Ramona and the Ramona Dam. This hike is a distance of about five miles, with an altitude gain of 800 feet. Midway along the Truck Trail, a hiking trail takes off to the right, heading south to Lake Poway. This is a three-mile hike, with an altitude gain of 500 feet. None of the trails loops around; you need to return on the same trail.

Sweetwater Regional Park
South Bay

Sweetwater is a long, narrow regional park that stretches from the Sweetwater Reservoir in the east, along the Sweetwater River, to Interstate 805 on the west. Both the Chula Vista City Golf Course and the Bonita Golf Course interrupt the county park, but it offers several choice spots in between for hiking.

Directions

Take Interstate 805 to the Bonita Road exit and go east. To get to the campgrounds and trails at the Summit Site, proceed east on Bonita Road. When the road turns north, continue straight eastward on San Miguel Road. Then turn left on Summit Meadow Road. This takes you to the park entrance. There is a $2 fee for day use.

To get to Morrison Pond, go east on Bonita Road only as far as Central Avenue. Turn north on Central, then east on Sweetwater Road. Pass Briarwood Road and you will find the entrance to the Morrison Pond Trail.

Description

The Summit Site has a large campground with corrals for those who bring their horses. There are a couple of picnic areas; one is actually a local park, just outside the park entrance. Two trails begin at the circular drive that takes you to the campground. The park ranger assured me that dogs are allowed on all trails, but must be kept on a leash.

Sweetwater Reservoir and hills are a South Bay oasis.

The trail that goes straight ahead takes you up to the summit, for a spectacular view of the surrounding countryside. Be alert for the sign leading to a private driveway, and don't take that path. The Lake View Trail goes off to the east before you reach the summit and leads around to the lake side. This trail goes uphill rather gently, and you find yourself above Sweetwater Reservoir and the dam. It is a great view of the lake. Dry grasses covered the hills at the time of my midsummer visit, but there were also some manzanita, wild mustard, and other scrub vegetation. Parts of the path are rocky, but it is still not a difficult hike. Along the trail, there was a lot of evidence that horses had taken this path before us.

Another trail goes west through the dry grasses, then north, providing a view overlooking the nearby golf course and houses. A long trail (nearly 5 miles) goes eastward along the southern side of the reservoir.

Morrison Pond offers a different kind of trail. This is a very easy short hike, with a wide, level dirt path leading from the parking area to the pond, which is surrounded by lush riparian vegetation. The trail wanders in the shade of tall sycamores, oak, and willows.

Otay Lakes County Park
South Bay

Otay Lakes County Park overlooks the Lower Otay Dam and lake, offering a quiet and scenic respite, plus some easy hiking with your dog. It is not far from new Chula Vista housing developments and the ARCO Olympic Training Center. This park will eventually be the end piece in a series of parks along the Otay River, forming the Otay Valley Regional Park.

Directions

From Interstate 805 in Chula Vista, head east on Olympic Parkway about 6 miles. Soon after you pass the gate of the Olympic Training Center, turn right onto Wueste Road. Continue along the lake to the end of the road. Here is the entrance to the park.

Description

At the entrance is a machine to collect your $2 fee for parking. It took my dollars, but did not dispense the ticket that I should have put on my dashboard. There is plenty of parking. Otay Lakes County Park is open Monday through Friday from 9:30 a.m. to 5 p.m., and on weekends and holidays from 9:30 a.m. to sunset.

View of Lower Otay Reservoir from Otay Lakes County Park.

Picnic area overlooks Lower Otay Reservoir.

You can take your dog anywhere in the park — on his leash, of course. The only exception to this, I was told by the park ranger, is to keep dogs away from the kid's play equipment.

There is a small hill of developed parkland, with picnic tables, gazebos, and children's play equipment. A grassy lawn covers much of the hillside, which overlooks the lake, visible through breaks in the line of trees along the parking lot.

A couple of gated roads are marked for emergency vehicles only, but you can hike these roads on foot (and paw) for some exercise. One of these goes up a nearby hill, with natural grasses and a few pine and eucalyptus trees. The dirt road up to the top switches back and gets a little steep, but the distance is short and this is not serious elevation. There are also a couple of foot-paths taking other routes up or down the hill. From the top you can see the face of Lower Otay Dam, with the lake beyond.

The other road is fairly level, taking off toward the south with a view toward the Otay Valley. This one goes about half a mile. It is not a loop, so you need to come back the same way.

Dos Picos Park includes a quiet lake.

Dos Picos Regional Park
Backcountry

Dos Picos is a regional park just south of Ramona, off Highway 67, deep in the rocky hills of inland San Diego County. This 78-acre park has camping, picnicking, a duck pond, and hillside trails that you can hike with your dog, on leash.

Directions

From Interstate 15, take Poway Road east to Highway 67. Turn left and continue about seven miles to Mussey Grade Road. Turn right (south) on Mussey Grade and continue the short distance to Dos Picos Park Road. A right turn takes you to the entrance of the park, which is on the left.

Description

As with other San Diego County parks, there is a $2 fee for parking for day use. A large, shady picnic area opens up just off the parking lot, with many tables and barbecues. The whole area is in the shelter of a grove of old oak trees. To the west lie the camping site area and a patch of grass for playing.

Straight through the picnic area, on the other side, is a unpaved service road that leads to a trailhead. The dirt trail leads gently up the hill, with large rocks placed neatly along the borders of the trail. Then you find yourself stepping up rock steps,

Stone steps at Dos Picos Regional Park.

up the hillside, with thick chaparral on both sides of the trail. Soon rock steps lead you down into a canyon and up the other side. From there, the trail goes off in two directions. To the right, it curves around and goes up to the top of the hill. The left path goes upward fairly gently, sometimes with rocks for steps, other times just an ascending dirt slope. Soon you are on top of the ridge, with a view of neighboring hillsides and Mount Woodson.

This is an easy trail. The only reason I have rated it easy to moderate is that the rock steps are uneven and can be tricky. You dog will probably take them easily enough. But you don't want to be pulled along too fast over these.

The trail continues on, still with the neat row of rocks lining the path. At one point, overlooking the park, you see the pond, which is at the east end of the park. Gradually, the path starts downward, becoming a descending dirt slope with uneven rock steps in places. It ends (or begins, if you choose to start there) near the placid pond, where you will find ducks swimming and flapping, dragonflies buzzing. You can walk around the pond, back toward the picnic area, or take another trail that leads off from the east side of the pond, heads southeast through a grove of oak trees, and over a wooden bridge. This path then takes you out into the open sun, before turning and rejoining the service road. These trails are not long, but in all, they offer some good exercise over the hillside.

Sycamore Canyon/Goodan Ranch Open Space Preserves
Backcountry

In the hills east of Poway and north of Santee lies Sycamore Canyon/Goodan Ranch Open Space Preserves. The Cedar Fire burned this area in 2003, and at this writing, about two years later, is in a recovery period. Here you can see chaparral and coastal sage vegetation filling in, while some black skeletal trees remain. There are more than 10 miles of hiking trails in Sycamore Canyon, and some of the trails are challenging.

Hiking trail in Sycamore Canyon.

Directions

Take Interstate 15 to the Poway Road exit. Head eastward to the point where Poway Road turns north. Do not turn, but continue straight ahead, east on Garden Road about a mile to Sycamore Canyon Road. Turn right on Sycamore Canyon Road and follow it to the end. There is a parking area at the gate. This gate is open from 8 a.m. to 5 p.m. from October to March, and from 8 a.m. to 7 p.m. from April to September.

There is also an entrance to Sycamore Canyon from Highway 67, but it is only open on weekends from 8 a.m. to 5 p.m.

Description

Sycamore Canyon/Goodan Ranch Open Space Preserves covers 1,700 acres, which includes an open valley and the surrounding hillsides. The Goodan Ranch site still has buildings from the working ranch that was active until the 1930s.

From the north gate at Sycamore Canyon Road, trails go off in two directions. The Martha's Grove Trail heads up into the hills on the east and a sign warns that it is a rugged and remote trail and it advises that you hike with a partner. This trail is a three-mile loop.

We took the trail that follows a dirt road to Goodan Ranch, southward from the gate. The road descends rather steeply toward the floor of the valley, offering a great view of the valley ahead. We had Bailey with us on this summer day, and the air was rich with the fragrance of sage and other plants. Even though many of the trees were charred in the fire, a great deal of vegetation is thriving, growing green at the base of damaged black remnants and sprouting from the renewed earth. The trail was lined with wild mustard, Laurel sumac, wild grasses and some wild flowers.

By this trail, it is slightly more than a mile to the Goodan Ranch. A little past the half-mile mark, we took advantage of solitary oak tree that stands next to the trail and paused in the shade for a while. Our furry pet was panting heavily and needed to get out of the sun for a while and have a drink of water. There is little shade in the canyon or on the surrounding hills, so be sure you carry enough water for you and your dog. Returning to the gate was, of course, uphill.

William Heise County Park
Backcountry

William Heise County Park covers a large area, more than 900 acres of mountain terrain near Julian, in the northern part of the Laguna Mountains. It has several different campsite areas, an RV or caravan area, and a few mountain cabins that can be rented, although you cannot take your dog in the cabins. There are also miles of trails. Large portions of Heise County Park were burned in the 2003 fires, but much old growth still remains. Hiking through here, you will see a mix of untouched towering pines and cedars, some burned trees still standing, and other vegetation in various stages of regeneration.

Directions

From where Highway 78 and Highway 79 join at Santa Ysabel, proceed south and eastward. About a mile before you would get to Julian, turn right on Pine Hills Road, then left on Frisius Road. Directions are well marked along the way. Frisius Road ends at the entrance to William Heise Park.

Description

The entrance road winds through old growth forest to various campsites and then past restrooms and a parking area near a meadow. Beyond the meadow is deep forest, with oak, pine, and cedar. We parked our car, crossed the meadow and entered the forested area. Past shaded picnic tables and near a couple of wilderness cabins we found an entrance to the Cedar Trail. This is a one-mile loop into the deep shade of the woods. It goes by Cedar Creek Pond and out into an area that was burned in the fires. The trail grows steep in places. The Cedar Trail was closed for about a year after the fires, but reopened in October 2004.

You can take your dog on any trail in Heise County Park as long as he is on a leash. Be sure that you both stay on the established trails, and clean up after your pet. Even though this is a wilderness area, others will be following along these trails.

If you follow the entrance road to the farthest tent camping area, you can pick up a short, half-mile self-guided nature trail, which connects with a longer trail that takes you to some scenic overlooks. The short nature trail also suffered some losses in the fires, as did the Canyon Oak Trail, a 1.25-mile loop trail across chaparral-covered slopes. The Desert View Trail is a 2.25-mile loop that covers some steep terrain and reaches Glen's View, with a vista toward the desert to the east. Weather permitting, you can see across Anza-Borrego Desert to the Salton Sea. This trail takes you through manzanita, chaparral, and scrub vegetation. While much of this was burned in the fires, you can witness the regeneration and regrowth first hand.

For more information, visit the San Diego County Parks and Recreation Department office at 2454 Heritage Park Row, San Diego, CA 92110. To phone for information, call (858) 694-3049. For reservations, call (858) 565-3600. Or, check out the agency's web site at: *www.sdparks.org.*

Taking a jog at Batiquitos Lagoon in Carlsbad.

10 Other Regional Parks

Other cities and jurisdictional entities in San Diego County have created regional parks and open spaces within or just outside city limits to allow residents to enjoy a bit of wilderness a short distance from home. The county's terrain provides ample opportunity, with countless chaparral-covered hillsides and canyons, numerous creeks, and several lagoons within its boundaries.

Rapid population growth is reflected in what may seem like endless new housing developments being cut into hillsides all over the county. At the same time, residents and political leaders are seeking ways to preserve parts of the natural environment while there is still time. Residents have let their local representatives know that they want to have natural areas accessible in their community, and the politicians have, to some extent, responded.

Some of the parks, open spaces, and trails discussed here have been here for a long time. Others, like the Carlsbad Citywide Trails Program and the San Dieguito River Park, are new and still being expanded. They all offer places, close to the city, where you can get away and experience the native environment. And with all of these, you can take your dog with you, on a leash, of course.

Carlsbad Citywide Trails Program

Carlsbad is still in the process of creating a series of nature trails within the city. At this writing, there are more than 17 miles of trails in seven different areas of the city, and more are being planned. I have explored trails in three different areas. For a complete, updated listing of what is available in the Carlsbad Citywide Trails Program, including maps, check out the city's web site at: *www.ci.carlsbad.ca.us/trails*.

| Hosp Grove Trail |
| North County Coastal |

Trail

Easy To Moderate

Hosp Grove has a series of trails up and around the hillside just south of the Plaza Camino Real shopping center. There are more than three miles of trails up and down hills and through eucalyptus groves.

Directions

Hosp Grove has trails on both sides of Monroe Street, with the western trails continuing into Hosp Grove Park. To get to the western section and to Hosp Grove Park picnic area from Highway 78, take the Jefferson Street exit south. Then turn right onto Jefferson Street and look for the park entrance to the left.

To get to the trails east of Monroe, also take the Jefferson exit off of Highway 78. Then cross the intersection with Jefferson and take Marron Road around to Monroe. Turn right onto Monroe and look for a small park entrance on the left.

The Eucalyptus Grove

The eucalyptus trees that can be found throughout much of southern California are non-native species, brought here from Australia.

In 1908, F.P. Hosp & Partners, in an enterprising move, planted 40,000 eucalyptus seedlings over these hills in hopes of providing wood for railroad ties for the expanding Santa Fe Railroad. The problem was, eucalyptus wood turned out not to be suitable for railroad ties.

The City of Carlsbad purchased the land in 1987, for this park that now covers 74 acres.

Failed railroad tie business left a wonderful eucalyptus grove in Carlsbad.

Description

Hosp Grove Park, on the west side, is just across the street from the Buena Vista Lagoon Ecological Reserve. There is a small parking lot, a playground and picnic area. Cross a small bridge and you get to the trailhead leading up the hill and into the eucalyptus groves. Trails take off from other trails. This is definitely a nature hike, moderately strenuous over the hillside.

The section to the east of Monroe Street is about the same, with many trails from which to choose. It would be easy to feel that you could get lost in the forest of eucalyptus, except for occasional glimpses of the shopping center or the street.

Rancho Carrillo Trails
North County Coastal

Trail

Easy To
Moderate

This is a series of about 4 miles of trails around the canyon surrounding Leo Carrillo Ranch Historic Park. Dogs are not allowed inside the historic park, but they are permitted on the trails, on a leash.

Directions

From Interstate 5, take Palomar Airport Road east several miles to Melrose Avenue. Turn right on Melrose and go to Poinsettia Lane. Turn right on Poinsettia, then turn left onto Paseo Escuela. This leads to a school parking lot. Note the right turn to the lower parking lot. The trailhead is at the end of this lower parking lot.

Description

From the parking area, trails take off in two directions. One goes west and generally downhill. It eventually crosses the canyon and goes up the other side, heading east. The other trail takes a left turn, going downhill gently, and continues eastward along the canyon. The trails are dirt, with some rutting in a few places from recent rains. The east-heading trail is wide and easy to walk with your dog. As it descends below the level of the parking lot, you come closer to the coastal sage vegetation, along with some large cactus. Oak trees rise to full height from the bottom of the canyon. Willow trees and sycamore are planted on the opposite side of the trail.

The trail heading west, going into the canyon and back up the other side is a more difficult hike. There are other trails on the east side of Melrose, through a much dryer part of the canyon.

Aviara, Batiquitos Lagoon
North County Coastal

Trail

Easy

The Aviara area of Carlsbad has 8 miles of trails, including a trail alongside the Batiquitos Lagoon. The lagoon is an ecological reserve managed by the California Department of Fish and Game.

Directions

From Interstate 5, take Poinsettia Lane east, turn right on Batiquitos Drive, and right again at Gabbiano Lane. This takes you

View of Batiquitos Lagoon.

into a neighborhood. Continue on until the street ends. There is a small parking lot and the west entrance to the trail.

If you continue on Batiquitos Drive, you will reach the east entrance to the trail and another parking area.

Description

A wide dirt trail parallels the north side of the Batiquitos Lagoon, up and a bit away from the salt marsh. A nature center near the west trailhead, run by the Batiquitos Lagoon Foundation, has printed information with details on lagoon ecology, birds, and vegetation, for a self-guided hike. There are benches along the trail for those who want to sit, breathe the salt air, and watch for Great Blue Herons or jumping fish. (Mullet, I learned, clean out their gills by jumping.)

Several small trails take off from the main trail. This is an easy and beautiful hike of nearly 2 miles from end to end. Joggers like this trail, because it is level and in good condition. While I was enjoying the trail, one man jogged by with his Golden trotting alongside him. Others strolled.

Aviara, Eucalyptus Grove Trail
North County Coastal

Trail

● ■

Easy To
Moderate

This trail travels along between a row of houses the hill and Kestrel Drive below. There are so many trees, eucalyptus and others, along the trail that you can, at times, lose sight of the houses and the street.

On the trail at Eucalyptus Grove.

Directions

Again, the entrance to Aviara is east on Poinsettia Lane from Interstate 5. Turn right on Batiquitos Drive and follow it around to Kestrel Drive. Turn left onto Kestrel. It curves around a bit, then start looking for the trailhead on the left.

Description

Railroad tie steps lead up from street level to the trail, where it takes off in both directions. It is a fairly level dirt path in and around eucalyptus trees rich with fragrance. You are within sight of the backyards of some houses along the way, but still surrounded by nature.

I could not go far on this trail when I visited, because parts of it were closed for repairs. There is only street parking for this trail. According to the Carlsbad Citywide Trails information, this trail is difficult in places.

Aviara, Black Sage Trail
North County Coastal

Trail

■ ◆

Moderate
To Strenuous

Black Sage Trail follows a canyon that cuts between two parts of a housing development and covers some pretty steep terrain.

Directions

As above, enter the Aviara neighborhood at Poinsettia Lane from Interstate 5. This time continue on Poinsettia to Ambrosia Lane. One entrance to the Black Sage Trail is to the right, just after you turn onto Ambrosia. I continued on to Docena Road and turned right. On a steep section of road that separates two groups of homes, pull over and park

Stairs along Black Sage Trail.

The entrance to the trail going north is at the lower part of this open canyon between the houses. The southward entrance is at the top of the canyon, on the opposite side of the street.

Description

The path going north starts near one of the private homes, and then proceeds down some curving steps and into an area thick with chaparral—manzanita, laurel sumac, and black sage. The path goes up; the path goes down. Up, then down. This is a short, but strenuous hike. Take it if you and your dog can handle some hill work.

The southbound trail across the street starts out more level. You are looking above treetops in the canyon and above houses in the distance. After a while this trail also starts down into the canyon and becomes more strenuous as well.

La Costa Glen Trails
North County Coastal

Trail
●
Easy

La Costa has a couple of trails that provide an easy walk, overlooking the natural canyon vegetation within the neighborhood.

Directions

From Interstate 5, take the La Costa Avenue exit east. Turn right on El Camino Real. To get to the La Costa Glen Trail, turn right on Calle Barcelona. The trailhead is on the right, at the far side of the canyon, or glen, as they call it.

To get to the other La Costa trail, turn left at Calle Barcelona, then left again at Paseo Aliso. Pass the canyon and you will find the La Costa Valley Trail on the right.

La Costa Glen Trail.

Description

These two La Costa trails are quite similar. Both are wide dirt paths, with a low green cyclone fence on the canyon side. There is planting on a slope on the neighborhood side of the path. The walk is level and easy, taking you near enough to the canyon to get a whiff of the sage and other plants along the fence and giving you a view of the lovely large trees growing up out of the canyon.

The La Costa Glen Trail is about a mile long. The La Costa Valley Trail is about half a mile.

Buena Vista Park, Vista
North County Inland

Buena Vista Park is a large (134-acre) park south of Highway 78, in a residential neighborhood in Vista. Most hours of the day it is a leash-only park, but the City of Vista has, at this writing, just started a new policy to allow dogs off leash from 5 p.m. to dusk, at this park only. If you plan to go, call the City of Vista to make sure that this is still the policy. The Vista parks department can be reached at (760) 726-1340 ext. 1575. At the time of this writing, Buena Vista Park had signs indicating that dogs must be on a leash at all times.

Directions

From Highway 78, take the Melrose Drive exit south. For the entrance to the north part of the park, turn right (west) on Shadowridge Drive, then left on Antigua Drive.

To get to the southern part of the park, continue on Melrose south to Mountain Pass. Turn right, then right into the entrance to the park.

Ducks enjoy the day at Buena Vista Park.

There is free parking at both entrances.

Description

This long park weaves in and around private homes, and at first glance, it looks like just small green spaces in the neighborhood. It actually stretches more than a mile from north to south, over a chaparral-covered hillside and down again. The northern section, off Shadowridge Drive, has a narrow pond with, at the time of my visit, many ducks. A wide grassy lawn has a few picnic tables and trees. Off to the west end a dirt trail leads up and over the hill, southward.

Entering at the south end of the park, at Mountain Pass, a driveway takes you down to another grassy picnic area, with play equipment for kids. A paved path from here leads into a secluded spot in the shade of sycamore trees, then across a small creek, and winds around through a deeply shaded area, rich with vegetation. The path continues on and emerges into the sun, with chaparral along the path, and eventually wanders back to the picnic area. This is a fun, very easy walk with your dog, either on leash or off.

A dirt path leads from here up the hill, going between homes, following the power lines right of way. This is a steeper, more challenging hike for both you and your dog.

Los Jilgueros Preserve, Fallbrook
North County Inland

Los Jilgueros is a 46-acre preserve of the Fallbrook Land Conservancy, and it provides a quiet strip of nature tucked out of sight in the southern part of Fallbrook.

Directions

From Highway 76, take Mission Road north, into Fallbrook. After passing Fallbrook High School, look for a sign on the right. It is easy to bypass the entrance to this preserve. The sign and driveway for Los Jilgueros are set back from the road, just

Wooden walk at Los Jilgueros.

beyond a bus stop. The driveway you are looking for is very close to the sign that points toward the Fallbrook Community Airpark. Turn right into the driveway and follow it to the entrance of the preserve. The private property signs refer to the land to the right and beyond the preserve.

Another entrance farther north on Mission Road does not having any parking area. There is some parking along Mission Road.

Description

A large circular drive and parking area greet you and two trailheads are visible, both heading north in this narrow but long nature preserve. The one on the east is wide and sunny; the one on the west is a little narrower and goes into the shade of towering sycamore trees. The paths meet at the north end of the preserve, forming an easy mile and a half loop.

Dogs are allowed on leash and must be under control at all times. A sign specifies that you not let your dog chase wildlife. You must stay on the paths and, of course, stay out of the wetland. There are boxes that hold a supply of doggie cleanup bags at the kiosks on each of the trails.

The shady dirt path winds around and leads to a wooden boardwalk, taking you slightly above the level of the lower wetland vegetation. At times the boardwalk becomes a bridge, goes over a creek, then goes back to being a dirt path again. After turning west, this path resumes its northward direction and parallels Mission Road, but about eight feet below street level. This gives the place a private, sort of secret feeling, hidden from sight, even while you can hear the cars going by. The riparian vegetation is thick in the wetland, and there is a pond partially obscured by cattails and willows.

If you continue northward, you eventually come alongside another pond near the end of the preserve. This one is not so hidden. Taking the loop around to join the east path, you pass some old abandoned farm equipment. There are a number of benches scattered throughout the area for those who have come to relax. The preserve is a favorite spot for local birdwatchers. Continuing back along the sunny path, you get a more open view across a meadow to the trees that border the creek.

Daley Ranch, Escondido
North County Inland

Daley Ranch is a 3,058-acre preserve for native plants and wildlife, open to the public for hiking, biking, and horseback riding. The City of Escondido bought the land for this purpose in 1996, to prevent its being taken over by encroaching development. Daley Ranch has an active group of naturalists and volunteers who lead nature hikes.

Daley Ranch preserve in Escondido.

Directions

From Interstate 15, take El Norte Parkway about 7 miles east to La Honda Drive. You will notice signs on the left for both the Daley Ranch and Dixon Lake. Turn left on La Honda Drive, and continue up the hill about a mile. There you will find the entrance to both Daley Ranch and Dixon Lake.

Description

The entrance to Daley Ranch is already at an elevation above the City of Escondido, and it continues upward from there. Near the gravel parking lot at the entrance is a large sign with a map of the hikes and rules of the park. There are six trails, and you can take your dog with you on any trail, on a leash of no more than eight feet. The sign also indicates the difficulty of each hike.

No motor vehicles are allowed in the Daley Ranch, but in order to allow people to easily get up to the Daley Ranch House, a free shuttle runs on Sundays, every half-hour from 8 a.m. to 4 p.m., taking visitors from the parking lot to the Ranch House. From there, you can pick up other trails.

Thick chaparral and coastal sage line some of the trails, filling the air with the rich smell of sagebrush mixed with other unde-

On the trail at Daley Ranch.

fined fragrances. If you look closely, you will find occasional low signs identifying vegetation: Laurel sumac, Yucca *Whipplei*. Other trails wind through woodlands areas of live oak and Engelmann oak.

Some of the trails are paved and some are dirt paths. The Ranch House Trail, straight ahead as you enter the gate, is paved and offers a hill to climb on the way up to the Ranch House. From there, the Jack Creek Meadow Loop is fairly level. In all there are more than 20 miles of trails to hike. Since this is a nature preserve, you must stay on the established trails.

Couples, families with small children, people with dogs, all types enjoy this close-in bit of natural southern California environment. Be aware that bikers and people on horseback might suddenly appear around the corner.

For more information about Daley Ranch in Escondido, you can check out their web site at *www.ci.escondido.ca.us/glance/ uniquely/daley/*.

Elfin Forest Recreational Reserve
North County Inland

This fancifully named park is owned by the San Diego County Water Authority and managed by the Olivenhain Municipal Water District as part of the Olivenhain Water Storage Project. The 750-acre reserve offers 7.5 miles of trails through oak woodland and thick chaparral vegetation. Much of this hiking is strenuous.

Directions

From Highway 78 take the Rancho Santa Fe exit south. Continue through San Marcos to San Elijo Road and turn left. This takes you into the new development of San Elijo Hills. As you reach what appears to be a town plaza, turn right onto Elfin Forest Road. This curves and becomes Harmony Grove Road. Just past the 6-mile marker, look for the entrance to the Elfin Forest Reserve on the right. The driveway takes you down to a parking area with restrooms, and a large kiosk showing types of plants in the area.

Description

From the parking lot, it is easy to find the the trailheads. Escondido Creek Trail is short and takes you to a couple of spots

Creek flows through Elfin Forest reserve.

Elfin Forest Recreational Reserve

Revised Dog Leash Rules

• Monday–Friday: Dogs are permitted off leash, but only at the top of the Way Up Trail.

• Saturday, Sunday and Holidays: Dogs are required to remain on leash at all times throughout the Efin Forest Recreational Reserve.

• Dogs must always be on a leash on any of the trails, 7 days a week.

along the creek to see the water rushing over the rocks. Sycamore, willow, and oaks shelter the creek.

The main trail is called, quite appropriately, The Way Up Trail. It is a steep path, with switchbacks, leading to the top of the mountain, a 1,200-foot climb. We crossed a bridge over the creek, and soon after we started up, we came to a tall box holding six walking sticks made of tree branches and the invitation to borrow one and please return it. I did. Up this trail you are very quickly over the treetops. The trail is rocky, with some loose dirt — I was glad I had borrowed a walking stick. The trail continues up and around, and at about a third of the way up, the Botanical Trail joins it from the left. If you make it all the way up to the top, there are picnic tables and restrooms, and some fantastic views. Actually, the view all along the trail is great.

If you decide to take the Botanical Trail from the trailhead, it starts out level and gentle alongside the creek. Then there is a crossing of the creek with no bridge. There are naturally placed stepping stones for getting across. While a person could fairly easily step from stone to stone, a dog might just decide it is easier to splash across in the water. That puts him on the soft dirt trail on the other side. While this may not bother many dog owners, I kept thinking about mud-caked paws, so we turned around at that point.

Lake Poway Recreation Area, Poway
North County Inland

This is an absolutely lovely park and recreation area designed around Lake Poway. Its grassy green hillside, with pine and eucalyptus trees, picnic tables, and play area all face the peaceful lake. There are boats available for rent, and fishing in the lake is a popular pastime.

Directions

From Interstate 15, take the Rancho Bernardo Road exit east. This becomes Espola Road when it enters the City of Poway. Follow Espola Road when it turns south, then look for Lake Poway Road. Turn east on Lake Poway Road and follow it into the park. Pass the first recreation area on the right and continue on the road to the lake. There is free parking for Poway residents. From April to October, there is a $4 charge for parking for nonresidents on weekends and holidays.

Trail winds around Lake Poway.

Description

There are several trails for hiking near and around Lake Poway. Dogs are allowed at Lake Poway Recreation Area on a leash no longer than six feet. In general, to keep dogs out of the lake, the rule is that dogs must be kept 100 feet from the water. However, a park ranger confirmed to me that you can take your dog on the level path that takes off from the far side of the grassy area and generally follows the curve of the lake. It is some 20 or 30 feet above the lake and separated from the water by lots of natural vegetation. Therefore, dogs are allowed on this wide dirt path that gives you an easy hike with your pet and a great view of Lake Poway. You should not walk your dog along the path that goes right along the front of the lake, at water level.

From the farthest parking lot is the entrance to another trail, the Poway Trail, which leads to the Mount Woodson Trail. Dogs are allowed on these trails, on leash, but both trails become steep and rocky, making for a very strenuous hike. You can, of course, take the trail part of the way up, then turn around and enjoy the view of the lake on the way back.

The Lake Poway Recreation Area is spread out enough to allow you to get in some exercise just walking around the grassy park itself. Or sit and have a picnic under a shade tree, with your pooch at your side.

Santee Lakes Recreation Preserve
East County

This 3-mile long park contains a chain of seven lakes, some playgrounds, including a "sprayground" for kids, picnic areas, and well over a hundred RV and camping sites. It is owned and operated by the Padre Dam Municipal Water District, and was designed to demonstrate the possibilities of recycled water for recreation. The water in these lakes undergoes primary and secondary treatment, filtration, and a high-level of disinfection. The water meets the State of California Health Code for safety for full-body contact, such as swimming. There is fishing and boating on some of the lakes.

Directions

From Highway 52, take the Mast Boulevard exit north, then east to Fanita Parkway. This takes you over Santee Lakes, 9310 Fanita Parkway, Santee. Turn right on Fanita Parkway, then right

Another sunny day at Santee Lakes.

again at Carlton Oaks and right into the entrance to the park. There is a $2 per vehicle day use charge on weekdays, $3 on weekends.

Description

At Santee Lakes, dogs are allowed only in a specified Pet Walk around lakes number six and seven, which are the last two. You can enter the park by vehicle at the main entrance, paying the vehicle fee, and drive back, or you can walk in at the pet gate adjacent to lake five on Fanita Parkway and Lake Canyon Road. A white fence separates lake five from lake six, and signs indicate that dogs are not allowed in the day use area, south of that fence.

A trail goes between lakes six and seven, and along the western edge of the lakes a somewhat rocky road parallels the water. You can look out over open water in places or past trees and clumps of cattails to see the lake and perhaps watch herons fly by. Ducks swim in their V-shaped formations, or climb onto the shore. On the eastern side of the lakes, walkers need to go around the campsites or wind along the camping road. Dogs are allowed among the campsites at these two lakes, as long as they are on a leash and as long as owners clean up after their dogs. There are four pet stations along the walk with plastic bags and trash cans.

You also need to be able to keep your dog quiet on this lovely and peaceful walk. If he is easily agitated by ducks, he might not do well here. Once again, sorry Bailey. I still have hopes that our training will ultimately result in a sociable walking partner, but that has not happened yet. But dogs who can ignore a lot of flapping, quacking birds would enjoy this outing.

Mast Park, Santee
East County

This 26.5-acre park is located along the north side of the San Diego River in Santee. It is right next to a small shopping center, but the focus is on the river environment, with a trail that follows the river, then crosses to the other side of the park. Mast Park is part of the series of parks being developed along the San Diego River, from the mountains to the ocean.

Directions

From either Highway 52 or Highway 125, take the Mission Gorge exit east. Turn left on Carlton Hills Boulevard. The entrance to Mast Park, 9125 Carlton Hills Blvd., Santee. will be on the right immediately after you cross the San Diego River. There is a free parking area in front, with an overflow parking lot at a lower level near the river.

Description

This park is narrow at the street, but deep. It is developed in the front section, with a basketball court, shaded picnic tables, restrooms, grassy lawns and a kids' playground. To the right, a

Among the trees at Mast Park in Santee.

paved path leads over a small bridge and then heads back into the natural part of the park. You may take your dog with you on the trail, but only on a leash. And be prepared to clean up after your pet. The wooded riparian growth is so dense to the south that you cannot even see the river. Tall oaks and sycamores shade the trail in places and there are benches along the way, where you can just sit and enjoy this piece of nature in the middle of Santee. Some of the undergrowth on the north side of the path was quite dry on this summer's day, but there was still plenty of green.

This park is home for the endangered least Bell's vireo, a songbird that is doing well in this river habitat. During the summer season, their nesting season, you may hear their calls.

This is an easy and pleasant walk to the back of the park. Cross trails intersect with this main trail. Some are dirt and some are paved. At the end of the park (less than half a mile) the path turns and crosses to the north side of the park for the return walk, by more shade trees and back to the start.

There is an equestrian trail that is off the main trail, so your dog does not need to meet a horse directly on the path.

Tijuana Slough National Wildlife Refuge
South Bay

Trail • **Easy**

This is arguably the southwestern-most point in the mainland United States where you can take your dog for a hike. Border Field State Park, which actually touches the border with Mexico, does not allow dogs. And the beach at the southern part of Imperial Beach does allow dogs, on a leash, but it is extremely rocky, and not much of a walk. So these trails at the Wildlife Refuge take you and your friend as near as the two of you can get to the corner of the country.

The Tijuana Slough is included in the regional parks chapter because it is not an urban walk. Like the lagoons in North County, it is a world apart, while still within sight of beachside condos.

Directions

Drive Interstate 5 south, nearly to the border, then take the Coronado Boulevard exit west. (This is not the entrance to the San Diego-Coronado Bay Bridge, which is north of here and much closer to downtown San Diego.) Heading west, Coronado Boulevard becomes Imperial Beach Boulevard when it enters the city of Imperial Beach.

There is a visitor center for the Wildlife Refuge near the corner of Third Street and Imperial Beach Boulevard, but the trails near here do not allow dogs. For the dog-friendly trail, turn from Imperial Beach Boulevard onto Fifth Street and continue south to Iris Avenue. There is a small parking lot and the trailhead for your walk.

Beachfront condos also have view of Tijuana Slough.

Description

The Tijuana Slough Wildlife Refuge is the northern part of the Tijuana Estuary, straddling the Tijuana River to the ocean. You must keep your dog on a leash and do not allow him to chase or harass any birds or other wildlife here.

The trail heads south for three-quarters of a mile, parallel to the Naval Auxiliary Landing Field Imperial Beach. On the day we visited, we saw nearly as many helicopters flying overhead as birds. But on some days you may see pelicans, plovers, egrets, and the threatened Least tern, among others birds. At the south end of the Landing Field, the trail turns west and offers a couple of other paths through this flat marsh area.

All the plants here are low, offering a view across to the ocean and the Coronados Islands. Since this is a marsh, I was surprised to see some vegetation typically found in arid regions — sage, even cholla — along with the saltwater marsh species. The National Estuarine Research Reserve System and the Field Stations Program of San Diego State University conduct research here of the varied ecosystems.

Boxers take a break at Cadman Park.

Part Five: Rex in the City

San Diego and other cities in the county provide many places for dog lovers to take their pets to play within the urban area. San Diego County has 20 dog parks, with more opening each year, where you can take off that leash and watch your friend run and leap and play with other dogs. There are also four leash-free beach areas for seaside fun.

Dogs must be leashed at all times

Clean up after your pet

Time for lessons at Morley Field.

In addition, I have included some special parks and walks around our region where you can walk your dog and enjoy the scenery and great climate we have here. Beyond those parks and public places discussed here, you can take your dog with you to most parks and on most city streets, as long as you use a leash and clean up after your pet.

Having fun at Nate's Point in Balboa Park.

11 Dog-Loving San Diego City Parks

Cities and communities all across San Diego County have parks or sections of parks where you and your dog will be welcome. Most parks allow dogs on leashes anywhere in the park, and some have areas specifically designated as leash-free, so your pet can run free, chase balls and Frisbees, and play with other dogs. The City of San Diego alone currently has eleven parks with leash-free zones.

Some of these areas have posted boundaries, but no fences. Therefore, your dog has to be trained well enough that you can trust him not to run beyond out of bounds. Bailey is, unfortunately, not suited for a leash-free park, and he may never be. But if your dog is cooperative and friendly, these are great places for both of you to enjoy.

Rules of the Park

In the leash-free city parks, dog owners need to follow the rules in order to make it a fun and pleasant place for all. Before arriving at the park, you need to know to:

- Keep your dog on a leash while walking to and from the leash-free area;
- Always pick up any deposits left by your dog;
- Make sure your puppy has had all required shots and vaccinations before you bring him to socialize;
- Check to see that your dog's shots are up to date as well;
- Have a current license attached to his collar.

Leash free in Balboa Park

Balboa Park, San Diego's beautiful urban park spreading over more than 1,000 acres, is located just north of downtown. You can walk with your dog on a leash over much of the park, but the leash must be no longer than eight feet. Three areas in Balboa Park are designated as leash-free: Nate's Point, Morley Field, and Grape Street Park.

Nate's Point
Balboa Park

This well-hidden spot is located on the south side of Cabrillo Bridge, that grand old bridge spanning Highway 163, connecting the section of the park that is west of the highway with the larger section east of the highway.

Directions

The best way to get to Nate's Point is to take Laurel Street eastward from Sixth Avenue. Laurel turns into El Prado once inside the park. You can park your vehicle on Sixth Avenue, or once you enter the park, you will see parking along Balboa Drive, the first cross street.

Description

Nate's Point Dog Exercise and Training Leash-free Area is on the south side of El Prado, just before it goes over the bridge. This is a dog park that is open for use 24 hours a day. All city dog parks have dispensers of plastic bags for cleaning up after your pooch, although you might want to take along a plastic bag, in case the supply is depleted. And, of course, the rules are posted.

Nate's Point has a broad area of grass and dirt, with plenty of room for play. Some of the dogs play together, others just ignore each other and play with their owner. Tall eucalyptus trees border much of the play area, and a canyon defines the boundary on one side. There are no fences at Nate's Point, just signs indicating that the dog exercise area ends here, so your dog must be under your voice control. Bailey would probably take off for parts unknown, but a lot of dogs happily stay and play within the area. This is a popular spot, particularly for after-work playtime for downtown residents and their best friends.

Morley Field
Balboa Park

Just northwest of the tennis courts in the Morley Field section of Balboa Park is another popular leash-free dog park.

Directions

To get there, take Park Boulevard to Morley Field Drive (a short distance north of the entrance to the San Diego Zoo). This takes you down into Florida Canyon and back up the other side. Turn in at the entrance to the tennis courts (right turn), then another right into the parking lot before you actually reach the tennis courts.

Description

Morley Field Dog Exercise and Training Leash-free Area sits at the end of this parking lot. The park is open 24 hours, but the parking lot closes between 10 p.m. and 7 a.m. For the detailed rules of the park, see sidebar.

Dogs play on a large grassy area here, with trees around the margins. Again there are no fences. Four-legged visitors need to be trustworthy. On the day I visited, dogless myself, this was a busy park. More than a dozen

Morley Field sun and shade.

City of San Diego, Park and
Recreation Department

Dog Exercise and Training Leash-Free Area Rules

1. Users must keep their dogs on leashes going to and from leash-free area.

2. Users must monitor and control their dogs at all times.

3. Owners must clean up after their dogs.

4. Aggressive behavior by dogs is not permitted.

5. Dogs must have current licenses, shots, and no contagious disease.

6. Puppies under four months of age are not recommended.

7. Spaying and neutering of dogs is recommended. Dogs in season are not allowed.

8. Parents must closely supervise children. Parents must ask permission from owner for children to play with a dog.

9. Excessive barking is not allowed.

10. Pet treats or food are not allowed, except as part of a Special Event that has a Park Use Permit.

dogs were romping across the lawns. There were dogs of all sizes — Labs, Golden retrievers, a standard Poodle, a Cocker spaniel, a Yorkshire terrier, and some unknown mixes — all playing together. A human would throw a ball, and several dogs would run to fetch it. Then the dog would bring it back to another person, as if taking turns. A sweet Labrador nudged my leg to get my attention to join the game. At one point, two dogs faced off and started barking. This sometimes happens. The owners quickly got them under control and the confrontation was over.

Grape Street Park
Balboa Park

Grape Street Park is a dog park in the Golden Hill neighborhood of San Diego, on the eastern edge of Balboa Park.

Directions

This hidden-away park area is best approached from the south. The simplest way to get there from downtown San Diego is to take Broadway east to 30th Street. Then turn left on 30th, which turns into Fern Street. Turn left on Grape Street and follow it into the park.

Description

The Grape Street Dog Park is surrounded by and fenced off from the Balboa Park Municipal Golf Course. The park faces a row of Golden Hill homes and a sign indicates that there have been complaints from the neighborhood.

It reads:

Attention Dog Owners. The neighbors of Grape Street are having problems with:

Downtown view from Grape Street Park.

1) The noise from cars, dogs, and people after hours; 2) Dogs running unattended onto their property; 3) Cars speeding down Grape Street. If we want to continue our leash-free zone, we have to be more considerate of our neighbors. Please be sensitive so our dogs don't lose their freedom!

This leash-free park is without fences on the street side, so owners need to be sure their dog is cooperative and responsive to voice commands. It was a quiet morning when I visited. There was just one dog and one owner, napping together on a blanket. The grassy park, with Balboa Park's familiar eucalyptus trees, has views to the downtown skyline. There are picnic tables and broad stretches of lawn for running and playing.

Dogs are allowed off leash at Grape Street Park Monday through Friday, 7:30 a.m. to 9 p.m., and Saturday, Sunday and Holidays, 9 a.m. to 9 p.m.

Dusty Rhodes Park
Ocean Beach

This is one of the newer dog parks in the City of San Diego. It is located in the triangle formed by Sunset Cliffs Boulevard, Nimitz Boulevard, and West Point Loma Boulevard in the Ocean Beach community.

Dusty Rhodes Park has wide-open spaces.

Directions

The easiest approach to the Dusty Rhodes Dog Park area from out of the area is to take the Sunset Cliffs Bridge southward from Sea World Drive. Once you get over the bridge, turn left at Nimitz, then right at the first driveway. There is a small parking lot.

If you are already in Ocean Beach or Point Loma, take Sunset Cliffs Boulevard northward past West Point Loma Boulevard, then look for the entrance to the Dusty Rhodes Park on the right. Drive all the way to the end.

Description

This dog park is a very large, one and a half acre fenced park. There are some good shade trees and plenty of territory still left for running and playing. Plastic chairs are available for owners who prefer to sit and watch the action.

There must have been a dozen dogs there on the day I visited, but it did not seem crowded. A number of the owners and dogs seemed to know each other. Sometimes a dog appeared to be waiting at the gate for a "friend dog" to enter. This is obviously a popular neighborhood park.

One owner told me that they need to bring their own water supply, and he put down a dish and filled it from a jug. Two other dogs immediately joined his, taking turns lapping up a drink. Some of the dog owners have joined in an effort to obtain funding to put in a water supply for the dogs.

Capehart Dog Park
Pacific Beach

This City of San Diego park was funded by the 2000 Parks Bond Act. Located north of Mission Bay on Mount Soledad Road, Capehart Dog Park offers two separate dog park areas.

Directions

From Interstate 5, take the Garnet Avenue exit west to Mount Soledad Road. Turn right, northward, on Mount Soledad Road and a short distance up the road you will see Capehart Dog Park on the left.

Description

Capehart Park is an off-leash park for dogs 24 hours a day. It consists of two fenced-in areas, one for small dogs and the

Capehart Dog Park.

other labeled "All dogs allowed." There were mostly large dogs in the latter area, but a smallish cocker spaniel was quite happy in there with the big pooches.

A small parking area runs between the fenced dog areas. The saplings in front of the parking lot will offer shelter some day, but this park is still quite new.

Each fenced area has a separate fenced-in entry, sort of a vestibule, where owners can stop, take off their dog's leash, then let them into the main dog play space. There are picnic tables with benches in each dog area for the owners, and water is available for thirsty dogs. As always, you need to pick up after your dog. The spaces have some sparse grass, but are mostly dirt.

Both the small dog and the all dogs areas were busy on the day I visited (without Bailey).

Cadman Community Park
4280 Avati Drive, Clairemont

Cadman Community Park, in the northwest part of Clairemont Mesa, offers a prize view overlooking Mission Bay. Coming through the Clairemont Mesa neighborhood, I did not expect this viewpoint.

Directions

From Interstate 5, take Balboa Avenue east, then turn left on Moraga Avenue. After it winds around a bit, turn left on Moraga Court, then follow it to the left as it becomes Avati Drive. You will see the park on the right.

Description

Cadman Community Park is not large, but it has a little bit of everything: picnic tables, children's play equipment, an athletic field, and an off-leash dog park. There is free parking in a small lot by the street.

Don't be discouraged by the sign indicating that dogs must be on leash at all times in this area. This just means that you need to keep the leash on until you reach the dog park section at the back of the park.

The leash-free dog park is a continuation of the lovely grass and shade tree parkland that extends all along the south side of the park. There are no fences here, so your pet really needs to be trustworthy.

Cadman Community Exercise and Training Leash-Free Dog Park has different hours for summer vacation. First, during the school year, it is open daily:

- 7:30 to 10 a.m. and
- 4:30 to 7 p.m.

During summer vacation it is open:

- 7 to 9:30 a.m. and

City view and trees at Cadman Park.

- 5 to 7:30 p.m.

The exception to these rules is that there are no leash-free hours on July 4, nor on Saturdays from March 1 to June 15, due to Little League.

Doyle Community Park
8175 Regents Road, University City

Doyle Community Park is a large neighborhood park with a recreation center, an extensive kid play equipment area, shaded picnic tables, athletic fields, and way in the back, a fenced leash-free dog park.

Directions

Coming from downtown, take Interstate 5 north and exit at Nobel Drive. Go east to Regents Road and turn right. Doyle Community Park is on the left. If you are coming from the north, exit at La Jolla Village Drive, go east to Regents Road and turn south on Regents Road.

Description

You will see the recreation center building in the front as you enter. There is free parking along the front of the park here. Take the path by the children's play area, follow it around the athletic field, and in the far back of the park you will find two fenced areas. Keep the dog on the leash until you get him inside. One

Big or small, there's room for all at Doyle Community Park.

fenced area is reserved for small dogs, the other is for any size dogs.

These off-leash yards have a few picnic tables inside, and scattered plastic chairs for the dogs' people. There is, of course, water for the dogs. The off-leash park is closed on Tuesday and Thursday, between noon and 2 p.m., for maintenance. Other than that, it is open 24 hours, but there are no lights here at night.

It is possible to get to this dog park by way of the street to the east of Regents Road, which is Cargill Avenue. A driveway off Cargill goes up into a small turnabout circle. Street parking is available on the Cargill Avenue side.

Torrey Highlands Park
Carmel Valley

This dog park is at the back of the Carmel Valley Linear Park off Del Mar Heights Road. This park is on a rise, above the level of the houses on the west, so a fresh breeze off the ocean keeps it refreshingly cool.

Directions

From Interstate 5, take the Del Mar Height Road exit, east. Past El Camino Real, look for Lansdale Drive on the left. You will see the tall power lines. Turn left, then left into the park. The first sign you see will be for Carmel Valley Linear Park. Follow the road nearly to the end. You will see the fenced dog area on the left, along with some parking spaces.

Convenient fountain at Torrey Highlands.

Description

The Torrey Highlands Dog Park is a large, one-acre fenced area, with a row of tall eucalyptus trees on one side, and plenty of space to run. It is one fenced area for all sizes of dog. It has the usual inner fenced vestibule, where you take your leashed dog and then undo the leash. This park has a new type

Zoey plays at Torrey Highlands Park.

of water supply for the dogs. The owner pushes a button, and a water dish fills.

Zoey, a chocolate Lab, was enjoying a game of catch with her owner when I visited. Soon three other dogs arrived and they all joined in, chasing the ball, chasing each other. Then a smaller dog arrived, and the large dogs allowed him to sniff around the park by himself. The owners all seemed quite happy to have this facility for an off-leash run for their dogs.

Rancho Bernardo Community Park
18448 West Bernardo Drive

This is the newest of the City of San Diego dog parks, open in summer 2005. This is a leash-free dog park, with three separate fenced areas; one for large dogs, one for small dogs, and one for any dogs.

Directions

From Interstate 15, take the West Bernardo Drive exit west. After it curves around toward the south, you will find the Rancho Bernardo Community Park. To get to the dog park, continue past the main entrance and past the middle parking section. Turn in to the last parking section on the south end of the park. The entrance to the dog park is at the south end of this parking lot.

Description

This is a large community park with just about any activity you would be looking for, from tennis, to basketball, to baseball, to lawn bowling. There is plenty of green grass and trees for picnicking. Now they have added the leash-free dog park at the far south end.

A paved path leads from the south parking lot to the three fenced leash-free areas. At the time of this writing, the new lawns inside looked flawless, but that may change after they have had some use. There are a few benches and number of small trees that will eventually offer shade. As one of the few leash-free dog parks in the northern part of San Diego County, chances are this will be very popular when the local dog owners discover it.

This dog park is open from dawn until dusk, but closed on Thursday from 8 a.m. to noon for maintenance.

In addition to the off-leash area, from the road that goes around the main part of the park, a trail takes off northward, joining the Piedras Pintadas Trail at the neighboring San Dieguito River Park (See Chapter 8). You can walk your dog on leash there, as well as in the developed community park.

Maddox Neighborhood Park
7815 Flanders Street

Maddox Neighborhood Park is deep inside the Mira Mesa neighborhood. It has the usual park facilities, with the addition of a fenced leash-free dog area.

Directions

From Mira Mesa Boulevard, turn south on Camino Ruiz, then west on Flanders Drive. Continue along Flanders and you will find the park on the left. There is street parking.

Description

Maddox Park is larger than some of the neighborhood parks, with an ample lawn area, a playground, and a few picnic tables. In the far southwest corner of the park is the fenced dog area. It has the usual fenced entrance space, where owners take their

Busy afternoon at the Kearny Mesa dog park.

dogs in, then take off the leash. Inside the dog park is a two-level water fountain, one at pooch level and one at people level.

It was busy on the afternoon I visited, with the after-work crowd taking their pets for some exercise. The dogs inside were, for the most part, either playing together or ignoring each other. On this day, as a woman approached with her dog on a leash, her dog and another large dog inside the fence suddenly started up a loud barking argument. She tried to calm him down, as did the owner of the dog inside, but they were unable to. So the woman turned, pulled her dog along and left. She was obviously disappointed that she could not take him inside the dog park that day, but she had no choice. That happens sometimes.

Kearny Mesa Community Park
3170 Armstrong Street

Kearny Mesa Community Park is a very large family recreation spot, with facilities including a public swimming pool, athletic fields, picnic tables, grass and shade trees, and in the next block, a leash-free dog park.

Directions

Coming from the downtown San Diego area, head northbound on Highway 163 to Mesa College Drive. Coming from the north, exit at Aero Drive and turn west. At Linda Vista Road, turn left (south) to get to Mesa College Drive. Take Mesa College Drive west to Armstrong Street, turn left, pass the main part of the park, and turn right at the next street. The dog park is at the end of this block.

Description

This off-leash dog park is a one-acre fenced area for dogs of any size. The same rules apply here as with any City of San Diego dog park. There were dogs of many sizes enjoying the park the late afternoon when I visited. It is a popular after work walk for neighborhood dogs and their owners.

Two people with small dogs walked the perimeter, while their little pups stayed right near their feet. An older lady with a walker was seated in a lawn chair, and her Scotty was resting in the shade of her chair. Other owners were throwing balls, instigating a chase.

Trees along one side offer shade, and there are chairs for owners to relax and watch their canine friends playing. Mesa College is visible across a canyon from here. There are two free parking areas for the dog park.

Cricket's Corner dog park in Encinitas.

12   Other Cities' Dog Parks

Other cities in San Diego County also have leash-free dog parks or parks that are leash free on certain days or during certain hours. Every community in the county has some parks or open spaces for its residents, and most of those allow you to bring your dog, at least on a leash. The parks described here have designated off-leash areas. Do not take your dog off leash at a park unless you see signs indicating that this is an off-leash area.

At this writing, the City of Chula Vista is completing a new park, Veterans Park and Recreation Center, which will include a leash-free dog area. It will be at 785 East Palomar.

Carlsbad Dog Park
Carlsbad Village Drive, Carlsbad

This mini-park is a fenced area near some major power lines on a hill in a Carlsbad residential neighborhood. It is part of

Making friends in Carlsbad.

Larwin Park, which is being developed as part of the Carlsbad Citywide Trails Program, extending north from the dog park.

Directions

From Interstate 5, take Carlsbad Village Drive east, past El Camino Real. The dog park is about one-quarter mile east of El Camino Real, uphill and on the north side of the street. You will see the power lines and the fenced area. The entrance to the small gravel parking lot is just east of the power lines.

Description

The Carlsbad Dog Park at Larwin Park is one fenced area, not large, covered with wood chips. All sizes of dogs play here. It is high on a hill, overlooking the neighborhood to the north, with a few eucalyptus trees along the back fence. There is not a lot of room for running around or playing long-distance games of fetch, but everyone seemed to be enjoying themselves. This is a popular after-work gathering place for dogs and owners.

There is a sign at the entrance listing the usual rules for off-leash dog parks, including keeping pooch on a leash until inside the fenced area and cleaning up after your own. Owners must be sure that their dog will respond to voice commands and not be aggressive with other dogs or people.

Orpheus Park
482 Orpheus Ave., Encinitas

This is a quiet neighborhood park that allows dogs off leash on certain days and only during specific hours. Dogs may be off leash here on Mondays, Wednesdays, and Fridays from 6 to 7:30 a.m. and again from 4 to 6 p.m.

Directions

From Interstate 5, take Encinitas Boulevard west. Turn right onto Vulcan Avenue, then right on Orpheus Avenue. The park is around the curve and a short distance ahead on the left. There is street parking.

Description

Orpheus Park is a small park of rolling, perfectly manicured lawn easing down to a playground sand pit. There is a small, covered picnic area. Another section of grassy park branches off from the picnic tables toward the south, with a paved path

Orpheus Park in Encinitas.

continuing around to a set of stairs at the back of the park, which lead to Union Street and the Paul Ecke Central Elementary School.

From the top of the park, you can catch a glimpse of the ocean in the distance. There are no fences within Orpheus Park, so when you take your dog off leash here, he must respond to your voice command. A sign warns that you must keep your dog out of the playground area and out of the landscaping. There are the usual rules about cleaning up after your pet and not allowing him to harass people or other animals. Your dog must also be licensed.

Encinitas Viewpoint Day Use Park
Cornish and D Streets, Encinitas

This is also a small, neighborhood park that allows dogs to be off leash on Mondays, Wednesdays, and Fridays, from 6 to 7:30 a.m. and 4 to 6 p.m. This park is just above old Encinitas.

Directions

Again from Interstate 5, take Encinitas Blvd. west to Vulcan Ave. Then turn left on Vulcan, then left again at D Street. Go up the hill on D Street. Viewpoint Park is on the left. There is street parking.

Room to roam in Encinitas.

Description

Viewpoint Park has three different levels, the highest being, logically, the viewpoint, with great views of the ocean, which is just a few blocks away. Steps take you from the entrance to the park, between some large pine trees, and up to the upper level. It is has a well-tended lawn and some benches facing the view. The whole park is quite narrow.

There are no fences here to keep dogs in. The lower level has a playground and a long stretch of grass, where your dog can run and play. On the day I visited, there were six white dogs, with different owners. It seemed to be the day of white dogs. They all got along well and chased around the grassy sections of the park. Needless to say, Bailey was not with me. Although he is nearly white, he does not yet play well with others.

The same rules apply here as at Orpheus Park.

Cricket's Corner Dog Park
389 Requeza Street, Encinitas

Sheltie surveys Cricket's Corner.

This is the only privately owned off-leash dog park that I found in the county. It is owned and operated by the Rancho Coastal Humane Society. They call it "Cricket's Corner, A Community Dog Park." It is only open on Tuesdays and Thursdays from 2 to 5 p.m. and Fridays and Saturdays from 11 a.m. to 5 p.m.

Directions

From Interstate 5, take the Encinitas Boulevard exit east to Westlake Street. Turn south on Westlake and follow it around until it reaches Requeza Street. Turn west on Requeza, heading back nearly to the freeway. You will see a sign for the Rancho Coastal Humane Society. Turn left into the driveway and follow it all the way back, through the gates and past the Humane Society building. There is a small parking lot right by Cricket's Corner.

Description

This is a quaint and beautifully tended dog park, with white picket fences, park benches, and shade trees. It is a fairly narrow, but long grassy fenced area, with a steep hill on one side. A sign indicates that puppies, small, and shy dogs can take advantage of the separate and secluded fenced area up and to the left of the entrance.

There is water available for people and for dogs. The usual rules apply here, plus one rule I had not seen before. They prohibit aggressive dogs and owners. Good idea. There is a box that you will notice when you exit for donations for the park. The suggested donation is $1 per visit.

Mayflower Dog Park
3420 Valley Center Road, Escondido

Mayflower Dog Park in Escondido.

Mayflower Park is a large, fenced, off-leash dog park, nestled by a rocky hillside in the northeast part of Escondido.

Directions

Follow El Norte Parkway east until it curves and becomes Citrus Avenue. Turn left on Washington Avenue, then left again at East Valley Parkway. This becomes Valley Center Road. Mayflower Dog Park is on the left, before you get to Lake Wohlford Road.

Description

Mayflower Dog Park has three separate fenced yards for dogs and their people within the larger area. At the entrance, by a large willow tree, you go through a gate into the area that leads to each of the yards. Owners should keep their dogs on leash until they are inside the fenced area. The areas are not labeled for size or weight. Visitors seemed to be choosing based on the dogs already inside, although most of the smaller dogs were playing in the first yard.

There are tables and benches, an occasional shade tree, and lots of room for frisky playing around in each area. A dog watering spot in each yard offers thirsty pooches a drink. The day I visited, in one yard a man and his big, black Newfoundland were resting in the shade of a tree. In another yard, a Jack Russell and a chocolate Lab were chasing balls and several standard Poodles were curiously exploring everything.

The rules state that you should bring no more than three dogs per person. As always, clean up after your dog and follow the basic rules of etiquette.

Pleasant surroundings at Poway Dog Park.

Poway Dog Park
13094 Civic Center Drive, Poway

This 1.7-acre dog park in Poway Community Park provides a popular social gathering place for dogs and dog owners. The park opened in 1996, and community volunteers raised the money for lights so that it would not have to close at sundown. Poway Dog Park stays open until 9:30 p.m. every night.

Directions

From Interstate 15, take Poway Road east to Civic Center Drive. Turn right, and in one block, you will see the Poway Community Park. Turn right toward the parking lot, where there is plenty of free parking. The dog park is behind the pool and the west ballfield. A sidewalk leading around the right of the pool will take you there.

Description

Keep your dog on the leash while you are walking around to the dog park. There are three large fenced off-leash areas. One is designated for small dogs. Each one has drinking water for the dogs to refresh themselves after a romp.

In a move of practical planning, the fenced dog park areas share a fence with the baseball field. There are benches in the shade of a row of pine trees and plenty of grassy, running around space for the pooches in all three areas.

This park seems to have a lot of regulars, who greet each other and each other's pets. Some of these dogs seem to recognize other dogs and are happy to see them.

Harry Griffen Park
9550 Milden Street, La Mesa

The dog park at Harry Griffen Park, called Canine Corners, is all the way to the back of this hidden-away neighborhood park. It is a good-sized park, with spots for sitting in the shade, picnic tables among eucalyptus trees, and a playground for kids.

La Mesa's Harry Griffin Park.

Directions

From Interstate 8, take the Severin Drive exit, north of the freeway, then immediately turn right onto Murray Drive. Turn left at Water Street, then right onto the first approach to Milden Street. A short distance in, you will see a sign and a driveway for Harry Griffen Park. Drive all the way back until you see the fenced dog area, and you will find free parking.

Description

The City of La Mesa has the usual rules for dog parks. Walk your dog on leash to Canine Corners and do not take off the leash until you are inside the fence. Clean up after your pet. Aggressive dogs and dogs in heat are not welcome.

A three-level water fountain sits at the entrance to Canine Corners, with two levels for people, one for dogs.

There are three fenced areas, with one specifically for small dogs under 30 pounds. There is a small pergola for shade, as well as some shade trees. One person was throwing a ball for a game of fetch, but most people on this warm day were sitting in the shade, enjoying the antics of the dogs interacting.

Wells Park Off-Leash Dog Park
1153 E. Madison Ave., El Cajon

Wells Park is a large community park in an older neighborhood in El Cajon, with an off-leash dog park in the back. The dog park is open from 7 a.m. to 9 p.m. daily.

Directions

From Interstate 8, take the Mollison Ave. exit south. Turn left on Madison Avenue. Wells Park is between First and Second Streets, on Madison, on the south side of the street. There is ample free parking.

Description

As with nearly all of the off-leash dog parks, the dog area is way in the back. A sidewalk leads you back, past the baseball field, to the pooch area. There are two very large fenced areas, one reserved for small dogs only. Each area has a gravel section and a grassy section, with scattered trees for shade. There is also a canopy over a couple of picnic tables. A three-level water fountain offers cool drinks for everyone.

On the day we visited, Lennon, a German Shepard, was happily chasing a Frisbee over a grassy knoll. Another dog hung out

Socializing at Wells Park in El Cajon.

with his people, by a bench, watching the action. I'm told that this park is very busy after work, when owners take their pets out for a stroll and a romp. The usual rules apply. You must clean up after your dog, and make sure that he is not threatening or aggressive toward anyone. Excessive barking is frowned upon.

On the shore at Ocean Beach.

13   Dog Beaches

For those of us who love dogs and love beaches, the two seem like a perfect match. What could be more healthy and joyful then spending a day at the beach, with the fresh, salty air ruffling the fur of your friend as he leaps after a Frisbee or splashes into the oncoming waves. Even shorthaired dogs seem to have a happy, squinty-eyed, wind-freshened look when they face directly into the sea breezes. Four beaches in San Diego county are designated as dog beaches, just for such enjoyment.

First, the Rules

Dogs are never allowed on state beaches, not even on a leash. Most San Diego City beaches permit dogs just between the hours of 6 p.m. and 9 a.m., and then they must be on a leash. Only the beaches discussed below allow you to unclip the leash and let him run free.

Enjoying the surf at Del Mar.

This kind of freedom is reserved for dogs that are well be-haved and respond to your voice commands. Aggressive and unruly dogs are not welcome. I have come to realize that Bailey cannot go off leash anywhere. His behavior is too unpredictable. I can take him to dog beaches, on a leash, but I must be prepared to pick him up and leave if he goes into a barking frenzy.

As with all public places, clean up after your dog. It is a good idea to bring a plastic bag to pick up any messes. Most dog beaches supply plastic bags, but you never know when the supply might be depleted.

If you are traveling on foot, you will need to use a leash while walking your dog to and from the beach. If you drive, use the leash until you get to the leash-free area of the beach.

Other Tips

Bring fresh water for you and your dog to drink, along with your dog's travel water bowl. Even with the brisk ocean breezes, the sun can get hot and anyone can become dehydrated. Don't forget sunblock for yourself. In southern California, it is possible to get a serious sunburn even on an overcast day.

Before you leave for the beach, if you are driving, think ahead about towels, brushes, or your dog crate. Plan how you are going to handle your possibly wet, definitely sandy companion when it comes time to leave.

Del Mar Dog Beach

This dog beach is easy to find. Del Mar Dog Beach is directly west of the Del Mar Fairgrounds, at the mouth of the San Dieguito River.

Directions

Take Interstate 5 to Via de la Valle and go west. Then turn left onto Highway 101, here called Camino Del Mar. The dog beach is the first sandy area on the right.

Description

The beach is bordered on the north by the James G. Scripps Bluff Preserve, and on the south by 29th Street. Parking can be a problem. There are some metered spaces along Highway 101. If the beach is not too crowded, you can find a place there. Look for the automated pay station, which handles payment ($1.50 per hour, with a four-hour limit) and gives a receipt to display on your dashboard. Street parking on the residential streets to the north is also a possibility.

The bluff was covered with blooming ice plant and wildflowers on my recent visit. Dogs are not allowed on the bluff, and people are warned to stay on the path in order to prevent erosion of the protected area.

Del Mar Dog Beach Rules

As with other public places, your dog must have a license and must be wearing his tag. The leash rules are a bit complicated.

On this beach, north of 29th Street:

- June 16th through September 14th, a leash is required.

- September 15th through June 15th, your dog can be off-leash and under voice control.

South of 29th Street and north of Powerhouse Park:

- October 1st through May 31st, a leash is required.

- June 1st through September 30th, dogs are prohibited.

South of Powerhouse Park:

- Dogs are allowed year round, but always on a leash.

The beach is bigger than it seems at first glance, with plenty of room to run and play. I saw friendly hounds splashing and running after one another. A Dachshund spent a lot of time industriously dragging a piece of driftwood up onto the sand. A Labrador had a game of fetch going, leaping into the water to retrieve the float toy thrown by his owner. He brought it back, and she threw it out again and again. Both were having a great time.

The waves were gentle and the water was shallow out some distance here, so the large dogs could run quite far into the water without going under. If you are standing nearby when a dog comes bounding out of the water, look out for the inevitable progressive shaking off, or enjoy a shower.

Fiesta Island

Fiesta Island is an undeveloped island in Mission Bay, not far from Sea World. It is a wide-open leash-free zone.

Directions

Take Interstate 5 to Sea World Drive and head west. Turn right onto Mission Bay Drive, then a quick left onto Fiesta Island. Once on the island, turn right; it is one way.

In the swim off Fiesta Island.

Description

The road generally follows the shoreline of the island, going around counterclockwise. You can pull off the road almost anywhere on the beach side. Read the signs for any restrictions.

Dogs are allowed off leash on Fiesta Island 24 hours a day. In the summer, the gate at the entrance is closed overnight, starting at 10 p.m., so you cannot drive on during that time. In other parts of Mission Bay Park, you can walk your dog on a leash between 6 p.m. and 9 a.m.

Like all islands in Mission Bay, Fiesta Island is nearly flat. Some vegetation on the inland side of the road keeps it from looking barren. The beaches of Fiesta Is-

What Was Mission Bay?

Mission Bay was originally a tidal marsh, which was named False Bay by Juan Cabrillo, because sailors looking for the entrance to San Diego Bay easily mistook this for the larger bay. In the late 1940s and 1950s, the City of San Diego undertook the massive task of dredging channels and building islands, creating Mission Bay Aquatic Park, with more than 4,000 acres of water and land for recreation. One of these created islands is Fiesta Island. Sea World, several resort hotels and marinas, and lots of parklands cover the other islands and shore.

land are a mixture of dirt and sand, stretching nearly flat to the water of Mission Bay.

It was not busy on a weekday morning. A family was playing with their two small dogs in one area. Around a bend and out of sight of them was a man with his three-year-old black Lab, Tonka. This puppy lived up to the Labrador's reputation as a water dog. Not only did he retrieve the ball thrown into the water, he dropped it on the sand and went back into the water to frolic by himself. Tonka stood on his hind legs in the shallow water and splashed repeatedly with his forepaws like a child in a bath. He was still splashing when I left.

Fiesta Island is shared by dog owners and water sport enthusiasts, who water ski and jet ski in the surrounding bay.

Ocean Beach Dog Beach

San Diego's colorful Ocean Beach neighborhood has a well-known dog beach that has been a favorite of many locals since its dedication in 1972. It is located just south of the Mission Bay channel.

Directions

To get there, follow Interstate 8 west until it ends. Then take Sunset Cliffs Boulevard south. Turn right on Point Loma Boulevard, then right again on Voltaire Street, and look for the signs to Dog Beach. As you enter the public parking lot, the beach is to the right, over a berm of sand. Parking is free. There are dispensers for dog cleanup bags.

Advisory

Some Ocean Beach Dog Beach users have noted times when aggressive dogs have attacked other dogs on the beach, and the owners did not make an attempt to stop them. While this is never predictable, keep an eye out for possible problems. If a conflict seems to be threatening, it may be advisable to pack up and find another place to play that day.

Description

Dogs can run off the leash here 24 hours a day, year round. This is a very popular beach, with lots of room for exuberant galloping across the sand. The beach is broad enough for a spread-out game of fetch or Frisbee. Its northern boundary is the shallow estuary where the San Diego River joins the sea. The southern boundary is clearly marked by another sand berm and a flood control jetty.

Riley is on the lookout at Ocean Beach.

Many dogs like to run into the waves or wade into the shallows of the river channel. On a recent visit there, I saw several dog owners throwing balls into the surf for their canine buddies to charge in after. The dogs seemed to love it and repeatedly begged for more. It is frequently the larger dogs that play in the surf: Labradors, Goldens, German shepherds. But this time, a scruffy little mixed breed joined in, attacking the waves fearlessly. Use your judgment about whether or not your dog can handle the strong surf. Southern California waves can get large and battering, and rip currents can be a concern.

The estuary on the north side of the beach is good for wading, with no waves and usually just a gentle current. It is a great place to cool off, without fighting the surf. It is fairly shallow — chest-high to a Yellow Lab when I was there. I always find it hypnotic to watch the interplay where the ocean tide meets the river current.

On the sand in Coronado.

Coronado Dog Beach

This is a beautiful, broad beach, with fine, white sand and an expansive openness to the sea. The northernmost part of North Beach in Coronado is devoted to dogs and their owners.

Directions

From anywhere but Coronado or Imperial Beach, getting to this beach includes a trip over the spectacular San Diego-Coronado Bay Bridge. The entrance is off Interstate 5, south of downtown San Diego. Once off the bridge, follow 4th Street straight ahead until you reach the boundary of Naval Air Station North Island. Turn left on Alameda Boulevard and follow it straight, then in a curving left turn, until it reaches Ocean Boulevard. Turn right on Ocean Boulevard and continue on until you reach the naval base again.

Description

Walking toward the dog beach from the street, you pass sandy hillocks and patches of ice plant on the left, and through the fence on the right you see the naval base golf course. Keep your

Sign Confusion

At the entrance to the access path to the leash-free beach is a sign reading: "No Dogs Allowed in This Area." If this sign is within about 30 feet of the naval base fence, look toward the ocean, and you will see smaller signs about keeping your dog on leash in the access area. You will also see containers with doggie cleanup bags. Stay to the right and walk along the sandy path to the leash-free beach.

dog on a leash while you are getting out to the dog area. The leash-free zone, once you are there, is clearly marked.

Out on the sand, the view is matchless. To the left, down the beach, you can see the historic Hotel Del Coronado, with its characteristic red turrets and cupolas. Sweeping around to the right, you see Point Loma and the entrance to San Diego Bay. Straight ahead is the Pacific.

There were perhaps a dozen dogs and their owners enjoying themselves on a recent visit. Some owners chose to keep their dogs on leash while walking along the beach. Other chose leashless freedom.

If your dog is skittish about loud noises, be aware that there may be landings of Navy jets at the nearby base while you are there. The approach to the landing field is over the beach, just to the south, and Navy fighters are very loud at close range. You can almost see the pilot's faces — they come in that low.

But when planes are not landing, it is a classically beautiful southern California beach reserved specifically for dogs and dog owners.

Along the shore at San Diego Bay.

14   Urban Walks For You and Your Dog

San Diego and other municipalities in the county have many lovely and interesting places to walk within the city. Some of these are in parks and some are on city streets. Discussed here are just a few suggested walks where you and your dog can both enjoy being outside and getting a little exercise.

As we all know, we need to keep our dogs on leashes, unless we are in a specifically marked off-leash area. We always need to be prepared to clean up after our dogs. And we need to keep our dogs under control and not allow them to disturb other people.

Seaport Village/Embarcadero Marina Park
Downtown San Diego

Seaport Village is a seaside shopping center that caters to visitors from out of town, but also provides locals with a great place to walk (and eat). Adjacent to Seaport Village is Embarca-

Dogs aren't the only animals on the lawn at Embarcadero Marina Park.

dero Marina Park, which takes you south as far as the San Diego Convention Center.

Directions

Seaport Village is located at the southwest corner of downtown San Diego, where the waterfront turns from a southerly direction to southeast, and it is directly across the Bay from Coronado. Seaport Village has two entrances; one at Kettner Boulevard, off Harbor Drive and the other where Pacific Highway crosses Harbor Drive. Both entrances take you to the parking lot. You take a ticket at the gate and have it validated for three hours of free parking.

Description — Seaport Village

Dogs must, naturally, be on leashes here. When Bailey visited Seaport Village, he handled the crowds just fine, but when we sat at an outdoor picnic table to eat food we had purchased at the cluster of casual restaurants (Greek, Mexican, hamburgers, fish, pizza), Bailey had his first close encounter with a seagull begging for crumbs, and he went crazy. That trip was cut short.

But many people quite successfully walk their dogs on the sidewalk along the low seawall here. Starting at the north end, you are just opposite whatever aircraft carriers happen to be docked at North Island at the time. As you round the bend, the dramatic arching curve of the San Diego-Coronado Bay Bridge spans the water ahead. This is a busy harbor, often with sailboats, harbor cruise boats, and Navy ships crossing paths in the bay. If you take the brick walkways through Seaport Village, you can window shop or watch the children on the carrousel. If you are there sometime without your dog, you can visit some of the nicer restaurants.

Description – Embarcadero Marina Park

The entrance to Embarcadero Marina Park is the same as the Kettner Boulevard entrance to Seaport Village. The continuation of Kettner enters the park just past the Harbor House Restaurant. There is some parking in this area.

Embarcadero is a grassy park, with shade trees and a sidewalk along the seawall. On many a windy Sunday afternoon, elaborately shaped kites fly jauntily overhead. The park loops around

Seaport Village walk has great views of San Diego Bay.

southward. This is a good park for on-leash exercise with your dog, walking, or just sitting together enjoying the fresh air and watching the boats.

Balboa Park
San Diego

Balboa Park, San Diego's largest urban park, is about 1,200 acres of parkland, museums, theaters, and the San Diego Zoo, all just north of the downtown area.

Directions

If you are approaching from north of downtown, take Highway 163, which runs right through the middle of Balboa Park. Take the Park Boulevard exit and turn left (north) to the park. One entrance is at President's Way; a left turn will take you to the neighborhood of the Aerospace Museum, the Automotive Museum, and Starlight Bowl.

If you continue north on Park Boulevard, you can turn left into the park just south of the Reuben H. Fleet Science Center, or at Spanish Village, the next left turn. Each of these leads to free parking.

Yes, there are quiet, uncrowded days on the Prado in Balboa Park.

From downtown San Diego, it is easy to approach the park by taking Sixth Avenue to Laurel Street, then turning right on Laurel. Once inside the park, Laurel becomes El Prado.

Description

While you will not be able to take your dog into the museums or theaters or the zoo, there is still a lot of park for you and your dog to enjoy. As mentioned in the dog park section, the off-leash areas are at Nate's Point, Morley Field, and Grape Street. In the rest of Balboa Park, you need to use a leash.

There is abundant room for on-leash running and playing across many of the grassy areas of the park. The Sixth Avenue side has broad lawns and shade trees. In addition, a large picnic area is just off Park Boulevard, south of the Reuben H. Fleet Science Center.

Or, for a different kind of route, you might want to take a leisurely walk across the Laurel Street Bridge to the main museum area along El Prado, past the Museum of Man, the Old Globe Theatre and the San Diego Museum of Art, then continuing on past the lily pond and the botanical building, ending at the fountain in front of the Science Center. This gives you a good look at many of the historic Spanish and Moorish style buildings in the park. And it gives your dog some exercise and time with you.

Balboa Park has some canyons and trails, particularly in Florida Canyon, on the east side of Park Boulevard. Maps of the trails are available at the visitor center, in the House of Hospitality on El Prado, roughly across from the Museum of Art.

Balboa Park's History

The land was designated as a park in 1868, and in the 1890s, horticulturist Kate O. Sessions oversaw the planting of hundreds of trees and exotic plants throughout the park.

The Panama-California Exposition, held here in 1915-1916, celebrated the completion of the Panama Canal, and to prepare for this international celebration, city fathers built the Spanish Colonial style buildings that later became the park's museums.

Soon after, the San Diego Zoo was established in the northern part of the park. In 1935-1936, the California-Pacific International Exposition prompted more building in similar styles, and the Old Globe Theatre was built to replicate the one in London.

Shoreline Park
Shelter Island, Pt. Loma

Tunaman's Memorial, Shelter Island.

Shoreline Park is a narrow strip that follows the length of Shelter Island, in San Diego, along the water, with views toward the downtown skyline, across to Naval Air Station North Island, and out to the sea, where the channel of San Diego Bay meets the Pacific. The park is just across the street from Humphrey's and the other resort hotels and restaurants that line Shelter Island Drive.

Directions

From the north, take Interstate 5 south to Rosecrans Boulevard. From the east, take Interstate 8 to Rosecrans. From the south, Pacific Highway from downtown will take you to Rosecrans. Follow Rosecrans west, into the Point Loma area of San Diego. Turn left at Shelter Island Drive and continue on, veering right as the road turns. There are usually parking spaces available along much of the length of the park.

Description

A long sidewalk parallels the water's edge at Shelter Island's Shoreline Park, traveling along just a few feet from San Diego Bay. A grassy strip with occasional trees provides parkland between the sidewalk and the street, with picnic tables here and there. As you walk, you pass under arbors of cascading bougainvillea crossing the sidewalk, with benches inside, in the flowery shade. Along the way you will see a statue of three fishermen struggling to haul in a large fish. This is the Tunaman's Memorial, built to honor those who died at sea while working in San Diego's formerly thriving tuna industry.

While taking this leisurely walk, you see boats and ships of all sizes passing on their way in or out of the harbor. If the timing is right, you might even see an aircraft carrier making the passage to the ocean. The buzz of activity across the way at North Island and the traffic of downtown San Diego seem distant. You can see a lot from here, yet feel away from it all, enjoying the fresh air and San Diego sun.

The ocean breezes pick up as you walk toward the channel the leads to the open sea. A small fishing pier hooks off from the sidewalk on the left, and a children's playground is on the right. If you walk all the way to the end of Shelter Island, you come upon the Friendship Bell, which was given to the City of San Diego by sister city Yokohama, Japan, in 1958, as a symbol of eternal friendship.

San Diego River Walk
Mission Valley

The watershed of the San Diego River is being preserved and developed as a system of parks, eventually to make parts of this river and its natural environment accessible to the public all the way from the Cuyamaca Mountains to the Pacific Ocean. In this book, we have already visited several parks that are part of this system. Inaja Memorial Park looks from a mountain viewpoint down the San Diego River Valley. Waters released from Lake Cuyamaca flow into Boulder Creek, a tributary of the San Diego River. Mast Park and Santee Lakes Recreation Area offer parkland near the river as it passes through Santee. The San Diego River also flows through Mission Trails Regional Park. And it eventually meets the Pacific Ocean at Dog Beach, where we watched the gentle interplay of waves meeting river flow.

San Diego River Walk in Mission Valley.

Various administrative entities, San Diego County and the adjoining cities, are developing individual parts of the San Diego River. The City of San Diego has already developed sections of river with trails for the public. And as long as it is a city park, you can walk there with your dog on a leash.

Directions

There are sections of San Diego River Walk going right through Mission Valley, behind shopping malls, next to condos. One entrance is at the northwest corner of Mission Center Road and Hazard Center Drive, going west. There is another section across Mission Center Road, going east.

There is also a section of river park on the south side of the river, off Mission Center Road, going in both directions.

To get to any of these, take the Mission Center Road exit off Interstate 8 and go a short distance north.

Description

The segment of river park at Hazard Center Road goes up a slight hill and under the overhead trolley tracks. A sign indicates that this is the "San Diego River Bicycle and Pedestrian Path." It is a paved path between condos on the north and riparian vegetation on the south. Breaks in the lush growth give glimpses of the river. This path continues all the way to the end of Hazard Center Drive. It seems very private and secluded, while being right in town.

As more segments of the San Diego River Walk are being developed, it will offer a longer nature walk right in busy Mission Valley.

For more information on the San Diego River project, check the web site at *www.sandiegoriver.org.*

Kate O. Sessions Park
San Diego

In addition to a statue and memorial to Kate O. Sessions in Balboa Park, commemorating her contributions to that park, a separate park just south of Mount Soledad was named in her honor. This is 79 acres of parkland wedged in the neighborhood north of Mission Bay.

View from Kate Sessions Park in Pacific Beach.

Directions

From Interstate 5, take the Balboa Avenue/Garnet Avenue exit west. Turn right (north) on Lamont Street and follow it to the park. Lamont Street turns into Soledad Road at the south end of Kate O. Sessions Park. A short way up the road is the entrance to the park, on the right.

Description

As you drive up into this park, you will find free parking and a remarkable view. You are high on a hill with Mission Bay clearly visible between trees, and downtown San Diego in the distance. This is a green, grassy slope with beautiful, large trees, not so close together as to obstruct the view. A paved path crosses the gentle slope down the hill and continues around toward the east and back up the hill. It is not strenuous, but enough to give you and your dog some exercise. Being so close to the coast and the bay, you get fresh ocean breezes up here. There are a few park benches, and lots of room to walk or just sit on the hillside.

The park has two distinct sections: perfect lawns on one side, and wild chaparral on the other. On the side north of the driveway and restrooms, a line of trees leads to a steep descent into a canyon, thick with native and non-native species of vegetation.

In several places, a couple of trails try to take off down the hill, then disappear into the thick growth. Outside the entrance, heading north and parallel to Soledad Road, a path follows along the canyon, overlooking the rich chaparral below.

With your dog on his leash, you can walk the path, dash across the lawns, or take off on the northward path for a longer hike.

Ellen Browning Scripps Park and Coast Boulevard Walk
La Jolla

There is a complicated schedule of when you can and cannot walk your dog here, both in the park and on the coast walk. But it is one of the most scenic parts of San Diego and is worth the trouble to figure it out. (See the sidebar for details.) Basically, it means you can walk your dog along this coastal walk, on a leash, early mornings, before 9 a.m. or late evenings, after either 4 p.m. or 6 p.m.

Directions

From Interstate 5, take the La Jolla Parkway exit west. This used to be called Ardath Road. Drive up, then down the hill into La Jolla. The road veers to the left, joining Torrey Pines Road. When you come to Prospect Street, turn right. Take the road down to La Jolla Cove and continue around until you find parking. You

Above the Pacific at La Jolla.

Hours for Dogs in La Jolla

Dogs are not allowed on beaches, walkways or parks at the following times:

9 a.m. to 4 p.m., November 1 through March 31

9 a.m. to 6 p.m., April 1 through October 31

You can walk your dog, on a leash:

4 p.m. to 9 a.m., November 1 through March 31

6 p.m. to 9 a.m., April 1 through October 31

may need to pass the Ellen Browning Scripps Park and try parking on Coast Boulevard. While you are finding parking, you will be glad it is early morning or late afternoon. Midday in the summer, parking is difficult to find.

Description

If you find a place for your vehicle near Ellen Browning Scripps Park, you can cut across the grass for a romp, or head for the sidewalk that runs parallel to the cliffs. These are not high cliffs; they lead down to low rocks and tidepools below. There are small beaches at both ends of the park. Walking along the park from end to end, you breathe in the fresh ocean air, look out to sea, and watch waves splashing on rocks. Scattered in the grassy areas of the park are trees shaped by the winds, some with gnarled bark like driftwood. There are a few picnic tables and barbecues available for use.

The sidewalk continues southward from the park, along Coast Boulevard. There are more pockets of beach along this route. One such beach is the Children's Pool, in the curved shelter of a seawall. During much of the year, this small beach is taken over by seals and sea lions, and signs warn you to keep your distance.

Oceanside Harbor
Oceanside

This well-hidden harbor is up the coast from San Diego, just south of Camp Pendleton. Besides being a marina for boats, Oceanside Harbor has a sidewalk all along its irregular perimeter, presenting a good long walk from one side around to the other.

Directions

Drive Interstate 5 north to Oceanside. Take the Oceanside Harbor Drive exit, west. This exit is very close the exit to Camp Pendleton. After you cross back under the freeway, Harbor Drive takes you to what appears to be a dead end. Turn left and go down the hill to the harbor. This entrance is at the south harbor.

Oceanside Harbor Village.

You can turn right, park on the street, and take off walking along the middle and north harbor. Or you can turn left, find parking in a lot, and walk the south side of the harbor.

Description

Turning right, you pass the Monterey Bay Canners restaurant, then look for street parking. There is a small park area, with grass and picnic tables following the waterline for some distance. Walking along the sidewalk from here you come to the spot where the harbor leads out to the ocean. The sun shining on the water and the fresh ocean breezes make this a pleasant place to walk for you and your dog. Continuing on, the sidewalk curves, still following the water's edge. You pass boats of all sizes, yachts to dinghies, tucked into slips, or tied along the side. The path makes a wide curve, passes the Jolly Roger's restaurant, and continues on a short distance farther. Since you cannot cross the opening of the harbor, you need to walk back the way you came.

If you turn left at the entrance and find parking in the south harbor area, you can follow the sidewalk along the water and marina on this side, past shops and restaurants, and eventually to Harbor Beach. Unfortunately, you cannot walk out onto the beach with your dog. Dogs are not allowed on the beaches anywhere in the City of Oceanside, with or without a leash. This south harbor stroll is much shorter than the one from the park on the other side. For a little more distance, you can, of course, do both.

Kit Carson Park
Escondido

Although Kit Carson Park is very much an urban recreation area, there are a few small trails that take you and your dog out of the city, at least mentally, for a short time. Dirt paths take you past ponds, surrounded by cattails and trees. The sounds from

Magic Circle at Kit Carson Park.

the athletic field seem muffled, and you can hear the songs of birds.

Directions

From Interstate 15, take the Via Rancho Parkway exit east. This will take you past the shopping mall now called Westfield Shoppingtown, North County (formerly the North County Faire). Look for the entrance to Kit Carson Park on the left, soon after you pass the mall.

Description

This is an active community park and a sprawling parkland of grass, shade trees, and picnic tables. Two birthday parties were being held in separate covered picnic areas on the Saturday afternoon I visited, and there was still plenty of open park for others to enjoy. A baseball game was going on in the athletic field. But when I found a trail that lead around a small pond just beyond the athletic field at the entrance, the surrounding trees and cattails made me feel as if I had left the urban park.

You can find this first pond and trail to the left of the parking lot at the entrance, and toward the back. It is so hidden behind trees and thick vegetation, you may not see the pond at first. The distance around it is not far, but it takes you away from the other park activity for a few minutes.

Natural area in Kit Carson Park.

Dogs are allowed at Kit Carson Park, on leash at all times. There were several pairs of pups, whose owners seem to be just enjoying being in the sunny park for an afternoon stroll.

To get to the second pond and a trail that leads to a surprising sculpture garden, you need to drive or walk around to the right of the entrance and back, away from the street. In the back you find another parking lot, another grassy park area, and another pond and trail. This one, the Iris Sankey Magical Garden Trail, leads to Queen Califa's Magical Circle. Follow the dirt path past the second little pond, past the picnic area, and up the trail to a colorful scene in the distance. It is an area of fanciful creatures created by artist Niki de Saint Phalle, with a bit of a mirrored maze at the entrance. Queen Califa's Magical Circle is open daily from 8 a.m. to 5 p.m. You can continue your walk for some distance past the sculpture garden before the trail ends.

Appendix 1
Trails and Parks

Appendix 2
Dog-Friendly Hotels and Inns

Many hotels will allow your dog to stay with you. Some hotels have a weight restriction for pets—only smaller dogs are allowed. Some charge a deposit or a per night fee. Occasionally you will find a hotel that requires your dog be in a crate if he is going to spend the night. The hotels and inns listed below all allow dogs to stay in the rooms. Policies can change, so be sure to call ahead. Most of these hotels ask that you tell them when you make a reservation that you are bringing a dog, and most ask that you not leave your dog unattended in the room. You are, of course, expected always to clean up after your pet.

A few of the hotel chains not only allow dogs, they welcome them, and offer special dog treats, perhaps a pillow bed, or other dog goodies and services. Starwood hotels (Westins, Sheratons) and Loew's may offer these extras.

North County Coastal

Oceanside

La Quinta Inn Oceanside
937 N. Coast Highway
Oceanside, California 92054
(760) 450-0730
*Dogs under 25 pounds
No additional charge*

Quality Inn
1403 Mission Avenue
Oceanside, CA 92054
(760) 721-6663
*Small dogs only, must be in crate
Charge $175 deposit (refundable)*

Ramada Limited
1440 Mission Avenue
Oceanside, CA 92054
(760) 967-4100
*Dogs under 40 lbs.
Charge $20 per night*

Vista

La Quinta Inn Vista
630 Sycamore Avenue
Vista, CA 92083
(760) 727-8180
*No size restriction
No additional charge*

Best Value Inn and Suites
330 Mar Vista Drive
Vista, CA 92083
(760) 726-2900
*Dogs under 15 pounds only,
Charge $100 deposit (refundable) and $5 per night*

Carlsbad

Four Seasons Resort Aviara
7100 Four Seasons Point
Carlsbad, CA 92009
(760) 603-6800
*Dogs under 15 pounds only, allowed in first floor rooms.
No additional charge*

Quality Inn and Suites
751 Raintree Drive
Carlsbad, CA 92009
(760) 931-1185
*No size restriction
Charge $10 per night*

Red Roof Inn Carlsbad
6117 Paseo del Norte
Carlsbad, CA 92009
(760) 438-1242
*No larger than 40 pounds
No additional charge*

Motel 6
1006 Carlsbad Village Drive
Carlsbad, CA 92008
(760) 434-7135
*No size restriction
No additional charge.*

North County Inland

Escondido

Best Western Inn
1700 Seven Oaks Road
Escondido, CA 92026
(760) 740-1700
*Dogs under 15 pounds
One-time charge $25*

Castle Creek Inn
29850 Circle R Way
Escondido, CA 92026
(760) 751-8800
*No size restriction
Charge $35 per dog per night*

Comfort Inn
1290 W Valley Parkway
Escondido, CA 92029
(760) 489-1010
*Charge $25 for big dogs,
$15 for small dogs*

Motel 6
900 N. Quince Street

Escondido, CA 92025
(760) 745-9252
No size restrictions
No additional charge

Poway

Best Western Country Inn
13845 Poway Road
Poway, CA 92064
(858) 748-6320
No size restrictions
One-time charge $15

Ramada Limited
12448 Poway Road
Poway, CA 92064
(858) 748-7311
No size restrictions
One-time charge $10

San Diego/Coronado

Coronado

Crown City Inn
520 Orange Ave
Coronado, CA 92118
(619) 435-3116
Pets allowed in some
rooms
You cannot leave your
dog unattended in the
room
Charge $8 per night

Loews Coronado Bay
Resort & Spa
4000 Coronado Bay Road
Coronado, CA 92118
(619) 424-4000
No size restrictions
One-time charge $25

San Diego

Best Western Lamplighter
Inn and Suites
6474 El Cajon Boulevard
San Diego, CA 92115
(619) 582-3088
No size restrictions
Charge $10 per pet, per
night

Bristol Hotel
1055 1st Avenue
San Diego, CA, 92101
(619) 232-6141
Dogs under 50 pounds
No additional charge

Doubletree Hotel Mission

Valley
7450 Hazard Center Drive
San Diego, CA 92108
(619) 297-5466
No size restrictions
Charge $50 one-time
non-refundable fee

Ocean Villa Inn
5142 West Point Loma
Boulevard
San Diego, CA 92107
(619) 224-3481
Dogs allowed in
downstairs rooms
One-time $25 charge for
up to 3 dogs, $50 for
four or more

Old Town Inn
4444 Pacific Highway
San Diego, CA 92110
(619) 260-8024
No size restrictions
Charge $10 per night

Red Lion Hanalei Hotel
San Diego
2270 Hotel Circle North
San Diego, CA 921108
(619) 297-1101
Dogs under 100 pounds
Charge $75 deposit
(refundable)

Residence Inn By Marrott
5400 Kearny Mesa Road
San Diego, CA 92111
(858) 278-2100
Dogs up to 65 pounds
Charge $75 deposit
(nonrefundable)

Residence Inn by Marriott
8901 Gilman Drive
La Jolla, CA 92037
(858) 587-1770
No size restrictions
Charge $75 one-time
cleaning fee

Sheraton San Diego Hotel
and Marina
1380 Harbor Island Drive
San Diego, CA 92101
(619) 291-2900
Dogs under 80 pounds
Do additional charge,
but you sign a waiver to
agree to pay for any
damages

Vagabond Inn Point Loma
1325 Scott Street
San Diego, CA 92106
(619) 224-3371
No size restrictions
Charge $10 per night

Westin Horton Plaza San
Diego
910 Broadway Circle
San Diego, CA 92101
(619) 239-2200
Dogs under 40 pounds
No additional charge

East County

El Cajon

Best Western Courtesy Inn
1355 E Main St.
El Cajon, CA 92021
(619) 440-7378
No size restrictions
Charge $6 per night

Motel 6
550 Monroe Court
El Cajon, CA 92020
(619) 588-6100
No size restrictions
No charge

Quality Inn and Suites
1250 El Cajon Boulevard
El Cajon, CA, 92020
(619) 588-8808 º
No size restrictions º
Charge $10 per night

La Mesa

E-Z 8 Motel
7851 Fletcher Parkway
La Mesa, CA 92041
(619) 698-9444
Dogs under 15 pounds
only
No additional charge

Motel 6
7621 Alvarado Road
La Mesa, CA 91941
(619) 464-7151
No size restrictions
No charge

Ramada Inn
7911 University Avenue
La Mesa, CA, 91941
(619) 466-5988
No size restrictions
Charge $25 deposit
(refundable)

South Bay

Chula Vista

La Quinta Inn
150 Bonita Road
Chula Vista, CA 91910
(619) 691-1211
No size restrictions
No additional charge

Motel 6
745 E Street
Chula Vista, CA 91910
(619) 422-4200
Small dogs welcome
No additional charge

Travel Inn
394 Broadway
Chula Vista, CA 91910
(619) 420-6600
No size restrictions
Charge $50 deposit
(refundable) and $6 per
night

National City
Bay View Suites
801 National City Boulevard
National City, CA 91950
(619) 336-1100
No size restrictions
One-time charge $35

E-Z 8 Motel (San Diego South)
1010 Outer Road
San Diego, CA 92154
(619) 575-8808
Dogs under 20 pounds
No additional charge

Backcountry

Borrego Springs

Borrego Springs Resort
1112 Tilting T Drive
Borrego Springs, CA 92004
(760) 767-5700
Dogs 20 pounds or less
Charge $50 deposit
(refundable)

Borrego Valley Inn
405 Palm Canyon Drive
Borrego Springs, CA 92004
(760) 767-0311
No size restrictions
One-time $25 charge

La Casa del Zorro
3845 Yaqui Pass Road
Borrego Springs, CA 92004
No size restrictions
Charge $100 deposit
(refundable) and $50
per night

Stanlunds Desert Motel
2771 Borrego Springs Road
Borrego Springs, CA 92004
(760) 767-5501
No size restrictions
Charge $10 per night,
per pet

Julian

Apple Tree Inn
4360 Highway 78
Julian, CA 92070
(760) 765-0222
No size restrictions
Charge $10 per pet, per
night

Julian Flat Top Mountain Retreat
Julian, CA
(858) 454-6733
No size restrictions.
No additional charge.
This is a cabin—a lovely
house in the mountains,
actually with lots of
windows. They also
have a fenced dog run.
Check their web site at
www.julianflattop.com

Pine Haven Cabin
Julian, CA 92036
(760) 726-9888
Charge $30 for the first
dog,
$10 additional for each
dog up to 3 dogs. This
is a cabin on a private
road, so they don't
want to publish the
address, but check out
the Web site at
www.pinehavencabin.com
and see how dog-
friendly they really are.

Web Sites

For information on dog-
friendly lodgings all
across the county, and
for lots of other pet-
related information,
check out the following
web sites:
www.dogfriendly.com
www.petswelcome.com
www.petfriendlytravel.com
www.peoplewithpets.com
*www.pets-allowed-
hotels.com*

Index

Olivenhain Municipal Water District 113
Orange County 17
Oriflamme Canyon 65
Orpheus Park 139, 140, 141
Otay Lakes County Park 94
Otay Valley 95
Otay Valley Regional Park 94

P

Pacific Crest Trail 33, 36
Padre Dam Municipal Water District 70, 116
Pala Indian Reservation 39
Palomar Mountain 6, 17, 40
Palomar Mountain State Park
    3, 9, 18, 37, 39, 40, 46
Palomar Observatory 26, 39
Palomar Ranger District xi
Paso Picacho Campground 40, 41, 42
Paul Ecke Central Elementary School 140
Peñasquitos Creek 76
Piedras Pintadas Interpretive Trail 74, 75
Pinyon Mountains 58, 62, 63
Plaza Camino Real 102
Plum Canyon 58, 60
Point Loma 128, 154
Poway, Calif. 90, 91, 98, 115
    Community Park 143
    Department of Parks and Recreation 84
    Dog Park 143
Poway Trail 116

Q

Quail Gardens County Park 70, 83

R

Ramona, Calif. 96
Ramona Dam 92
Rancho Bernardo 74
Rancho Bernardo Community Park 76, 133
Rancho Coastal Humane Society 141
Rancho Guajome Adobe 85
Riverside County 17, 35

S

Salton Sea 42, 57, 100
San Bernardino National Forest 24
San Diego Bay 154, 155, 160
San Diego, Calif. 71, 76, 77, 79
    Park and Recreation Department xi, 81
San Diego Convention Center 156
San Diego County Parks and Recreation
    Department 90
San Diego County Water Authority 113
San Diego Natural History Museum
    20, 21, 78
San Diego River 80, 118, 161, 162
San Diego River Bicycle and Pedestrian Path
    162
San Diego River Valley 29, 161
San Diego River Walk 161, 162

San Diego State University 120
San Diego Wild Animal Park 72
San Diego Zoo 125
San Diego-Coronado Bay Bridge
    119, 153, 157
San Dieguito River 74, 149
San Dieguito River Park 69, 72, 74, 101
San Elijo Lagoon 86
    Ecological Reserve 70
    Nature Center 86
San Felipe Creek 57, 59
San Felipe Stage Station Site 62
San Jacinto Mountains 17
San Pasqual Valley 72, 73
San Pasqual-Clevenger Canyon 72
    Open Space Park 69, 72
San Ysidro Mountains 51, 52, 53
Santa Ana Mountains 17
Santa Fe Railroad 75
Santa Ysabel, Calif. 28, 99
Santa Ysabel Open Space Preserve 70, 83
Santa Ysabel Valley 29
Santee, Calif. 98, 116, 118
Santee Lakes 70, 117
    Recreation Area 161
Sea World 150, 151
Seaport Village 155, 156, 157
Sessions, Kate O. 162
Shelter Island 160
Shoreline Park 160
South Fortuna Mountain 80
Spanish Village 158
Stag Cove 60
Stonewall Mine 43, 44
Stonewall Peak 42
Summit Site 92
Sweetwater Reservoir 93
Sweetwater River 92
Sycamore Canyon 83, 98
Sycamore Canyon/Goodan Ranch Open Space
    Preserves 70, 98

T

Tamarisk Grove 60
Tecolote Canyon 77, 78
    Natural Park 69, 78
Tecolote Creek 79
Thimble Trail 51
Tijuana River 120
    Estuary 120
    Slough 120
        National Wildlife Refuge 119, 120
        National Wildlife Refuge Visitors Center
        120
Torrey Highlands Park 132, 133

V

Vallecito Stage Station 67
Vallecito Valley 61
Veterans Park and Recreation Center 137
Viewpoint Park 140
Volcan Mountain 74

Open Space Preserve 70, 83

SUNBELT
PUBLICATIONS

"Adventures in the Natural History and Cultural Heritage of the Californias"

Series Editor—Lowell Lindsay

Southern California Series:

Orange County Place Names A to Z	Brigandi
Fire, Chaparral, and Survival in Southern California	Halsey
California's El Camino Real and Its Historic Bells	Kurillo
Mission Memoirs: Reflections on California's Past	Ruscin
Campgrounds of Santa Barbara and Ventura Counties	Tyler
Campgrounds of Los Angeles and Orange Counties	Tyler
The Sugar Bear Story: A Chumash Tale	Yee/Ygnacio-De Soto

California Desert Series:

Fossil Treasures of the Anza-Borrego Desert	Jefferson, Lindsay, eds.
Anza-Borrego A To Z: People, Places, and Things	D. Lindsay
Marshal South and the Ghost Mountain Chronicles	D. Lindsay
The Anza-Borrego Desert Region (Wilderness Press)	L. and D. Lindsay
Palm Springs Oasis: A Photographic Essay	Lawson
Palm Springs Legends	Niemann
Desert Lore of Southern California	Pepper
Peaks, Palms, and Picnics: Journeys in Coachella Valley	Pyle

Baja California/Mexico Series:

Cave Paintings of Baja California	Crosby
Gateway to Alta California	Crosby
The Kelemen Journals	Kelemen
Journey with a Baja Burro	Mackintosh
Houses of Los Cabos (Amaroma)	Martinez, ed.
Houses by the Sea (Amaroma)	Martinez, ed.
Baja Legends: Historic Characters, Events, Locations	Niemann
Loreto, Baja California: First Capital (Tio Press)	O'Neil
Spanish Lingo for the Savvy Gringo	Reid
Tequila, Lemon, and Salt	Reveles
Mexican Slang Plus Graffiti	Robinson

San Diego Series:

SUNBELT PUBLICATIONS

Incorporated in 1988 with roots in publishing since 1973, Sunbelt produces and distributes natural science and outdoor guidebooks, regional histories and reference books, plus pictorials and stories that celebrate the land and its people.

Our publishing program focuses on the Californias which are today three states in two nations sharing one Pacific shore. Sunbelt books help to discover and conserve the natural and historical heritage of unique regions on the frontiers of adventure and learning. Our books guide readers into distinctive communities and special places, both natural and man-made.

We carry hundreds of books on San Diego and southern California!

Visit us online at:

www.sunbeltbooks.com